ULTIMATE
CHRISTMAS

ULTIMATE
CHRISTMAS

JANE NEWDICK

DORLING KINDERSLEY

London • New York
Sydney • Moscow

A Dorling Kindersley Book
www.dk.com

Project Editor
Annabel Martin

Art Editors
Kate Scott
Kylie Mulquin

Senior Art Editor
Tracey Clarke

Food Editor
Alexa Stace

Photography
Dave King

Food Photography
Martin Brigdale

Recipes
Janice Murfitt

Managing Editor
Susannah Marriott

Managing Art Editor
Toni Kay

D.T.P. Designer
Karen Ruane

Production Controller
Patricia Harrington

First published in Great Britain in 1996 by
Dorling Kindersley Limited,
9 Henrietta Street, London WC2E 8PS

Reprinted (twice) in 1996
Reprinted in 1997

Copyright © 1996 Dorling Kindersley Limited, London

Text copyright © 1996 Jane Newdick

First published in paperback 1999

A CIP catalogue record for this book is available from
the British Library.

ISBN 0 7513 0742 4

Reproduced by Colourscan, Singapore

Printed and bound by
C & C Offset Printing Co., Ltd., Hong Kong

CONTENTS

INTRODUCTION

THESE DAYS IT WOULD BE VERY EASY to get everything you need for a perfect Christmas in one expensive and exhausting shopping spree. For two or three months each year, stores try to tempt us with a bewildering choice of Christmas items: food from around the world, sophisticated decorations, glamorous gifts, even ready-decorated trees complete with lights. It seems we have come a long way from the days of decorating the house with a branch of evergreen and slipping a tangerine and a wooden toy into a child's stocking, but along this route to such plenty we are at risk of losing the very pleasures and delights of getting involved in the real preparations for festivity. The satisfaction of making and giving gifts, cooking family recipes, carefully unpacking heirloom decorations, or weaving a simple door wreath is immeasurable, and it all builds up toward the excitement of the day itself. In a rush to have everything bigger, newer or better we lose out by ignoring our own creativity and forgetting that a gift, home-made and carefully wrapped, will charm the recipient a hundred times more than a glossy impersonal shop-bought present.

Home-made, however, does not have to mean quaint and unsophisticated – today we have such a superb choice of ingredients and materials that making things for Christmas has never been easier. There are luxurious papers, glossy paints, vivid fabrics, ornate beads, gold leaf, gilding creams, fresh and preserved fruit, leaves and flowers, thin, fat, short and tall candles in all sorts of colours, intricate ribbons and much, much more.

Another important part of Christmas is the food we eat to celebrate with friends and family. The availability of ingredients from around the world makes Christmas an excellent time to experiment with recipes from other cultures in addition to cooking the well-loved dishes from our own countries that do so much to give us a sense of continuity and security in our often hectic lives.

While many of us do not have the confidence to make everyday things ourselves, presuming bought to be best, there does seem to be more of a tradition for having a go with Christmas decorations, whether a table centrepiece with candles and flowers, greetings cards decorated with a stamped motif, or just a personalized gift wrapping. The secret is to begin by attempting things that come easily to you: if you can sew, try making some luxurious fabric tree decorations; while if the most you can handle is a tube of glue, stick seeds to a cotton ball to make beautiful natural baubles. The cooks among us would probably prefer to create a clutch of biscuit shapes to thread as tree decorations, but even the most untalented creators can string fruit and popcorn into garlands to wind through the tree's branches.

Small successes help you gain the confidence to experiment more, and to enjoy the process of making and doing, discovering a great pleasure in working at your own speed surrounded by exquisite ingredients. If you have invested your precious time, love and creativity into the projects they cannot fail to be extra-special. Good luck in making one or all of the ideas in the book – may this Christmas be the first "ultimate Christmas" of many.

Jane Newdick

THE HISTORY OF CHRISTMAS

A CHILD DISCOVERING the delights of Christmas for the first time is presented with a wonderful array of good things: trees with sparkling lights, carol singers, rich food such as iced cakes and biscuits, presents tucked into bulging stockings and days of excitement and parties. The modern holiday is in fact a cornucopia of widely different traditions, all combined into what we think of as Christmas. Some traditions come from religious sources or social customs, while others have their origins in folklore and magic. Over the centuries, the secular and religious traditions have become entwined and embellished to create a fascinating ritual.

Deck the Halls
Victorian Christmas cards show homes adorned with evergreen boughs

CHRISTMAS DAY

Feasts held in deep midwinter to celebrate the winter solstice, or shortest day, were common long before Christianity, and have been traced across Europe to ancient Babylon and Egypt. One of the most notable was the Roman Saturnalia, from 17 to 24 December.
The Christian church chose various dates for Christ's birthday before settling finally on 25 December, a deliberate substitution for the pagan festival celebrating the rebirth of light in the winter gloom. Some of the rituals and customs used in the pagan celebrations, such as the "greening" of public buildings and houses with branches, were also rapidly absorbed by the Christian church.

THE TREE AND EVERGREENS

Tree worship dates back to prehistoric times, and the Christmas tree probably has pagan origins, being an evergreen and thus the one tree in the forest with the promise of survival to spring. Fir trees decorated with apples, paper flowers and candles were introduced into Britain by German immigrants, and then made popular in the 19th century by Prince Albert, the German-born husband of Queen Victoria.

He also introduced decorations made from spun glass, miniature wooden toys and paper ornaments. By the end of the 19th century, decorations were being made commercially, and now most people buy mass-produced baubles, tinsel and other decorations rather than making their own.

Green boughs, mistletoe and holly were all used in pagan celebrations long before the advent of Christianity. Mistletoe was particularly prized by the Celtic Druids, who believed that it warded off evil and promoted fertility. Other cultures used it too, including the Greeks and Romans, and in Norse mythology it represented peace. While holly was adopted by the Christian church – its red berries symbolizing Christ's blood – mistletoe with its powerful pagan symbolism was banned in churches, though no doorway is complete without a bunch of mistletoe or a kissing bough.

Salt Dough Crowns
(See pages 20-21)
Decorate a traditional tree with home-made salt dough shapes

CARDS AND GIFTS

The ancient Romans gave lavish gifts to each other during the feast days of the Saturnalia, but it took many more centuries to see a widespread adoption of this present-giving. Not until the late 19th century and the beginnings of consumerism did it become usual to give and receive gifts. Originally, these simple home-made offerings were unwrapped, but they later came to be elaborately presented in special boxes and papers to signify the season.

Traditional Christmas Card
The sending of Christmas cards dates back to the mid-19th century

Cards were yet another Victorian addition to Christmas. At first they were quite unseasonal in their designs, occasionally bawdy and usually sentimental. Images such as the Christmas robin and snow scenes became popular with the advent of colour printing. In 1843 Henry Cole, the director of the Victoria and Albert Museum, produced the first commercial cards. The introduction of the penny post in Britain meant that card-sending gained momentum, and people were encouraged to "post early for Christmas".

THE ORIGIN OF SANTA

Santa Claus, Father Christmas, St Nicholas and Sinterklaas are basically all the same person, descended from the Roman King of the Saturnalia. The original St Nicholas was a 4th-century saint. His cult became popular in the Middle Ages, and in Switzerland, Germany and the Netherlands he was linked with gift-giving on his feast day, 6 December. The image of a white-bearded man in a red and white suit is very recent. A century ago, Santa Claus was usually depicted in a long brown robe or furs carrying a cross and wine flask with a holly crown on his head. In 1885 a Boston printer, Louis Prang, first devised the red-suited Santa and this theme was later developed by the Coca-Cola ad artist Haddon Sundblom in the 1930s, producing the modern image of a jolly character in a red suit trimmed with white fur. The reindeer that carry Santa Claus through the frosty night probably came from stories of the Norse god Woden who rode through the sky with reindeer and 42 ghostly huntsmen. Clement Moore's famous poem *A Visit from St Nicholas* ("Twas the night before Christmas") sealed the image of Santa Claus, his reindeer and the magical flying sleigh loaded with sacks of presents.

Santa Claus
Santa started out in brown robes, but is recognized today by his red suit and white beard

CUSTOMS AND TRADITIONS

There are endless games and pastimes, quirky customs and odd traditions that happen only at this time of year. Many have their origins far in the past, such as the yule log. To most people this is now a delicious chocolate cake shaped like a log of wood, but originally the yule log was dragged home from the woods with much ceremony and then lit on Christmas Eve to symbolize the sun and its warmth.

A picture of a man was once chalked on the log in parts of Britain, perhaps a long-forgotten reference to ancient sacrifices made at the winter solstice. An Englishman called Tom Smith invented the tube-shaped cracker as we know it, with a fire cracker inside to produce the bang. The paper hat in the cracker may be related to the hats worn in Tudor times by the Lords of Misrule, who were the leaders of the Christmas revels.

Games, singing and dancing were all seasonal entertainments and still are, albeit in very different forms. People gathered together on the dark nights of the winter solstice centuries ago and broke out into merriment and wild behaviour, fuelled with plenty of food and drink. Not much changes! Pantomimes too have a long tradition, and usually include role reversal of the sexes and of authority, and dressing-up. The modern version can be traced through Saturnalian festivities and mumming plays up to the 18th-century harlequinades.

Tree Baubles
Coloured glass baubles are designed to catch the light

FOOD AND FEASTS

The concentration on food and feasting at Christmas is hardly surprising – centuries ago before the days of canning and freezing it was difficult to survive the winter without stores of preserved food. Summer preserves and the last of the fresh food were brought out for a festive feast, while hardship was forgotten for a brief time of rest, celebration and merry-making. Some traditional Christmas recipes hark back to those times when foods such as dried fruit and nuts were luxuries saved for feasting. Spices and flavourings are important in many of these recipes, bringing echoes of earlier dishes in which these precious ingredients were gathered from all over the known world. Most countries have dishes that are special to this time, such as the heavy fruit cakes and round Christmas puddings from Britain, the roast goose from Germany stuffed with apples and nuts, and the spiced cakes, biscuits and breads of central Europe.

Roast Turkey with Cornbread Stuffing
(See page 159 for recipe)
Serve with cranberries, blueberries, pumpkin and roasted chestnuts

A GALLERY OF CHRISTMAS TREES

The first indoor Christmas trees were cut from
the forest and decorated only sparsely, but today
there is a bewildering choice of trees and
elaborate decorations available to suit all
tastes. Whether you opt for a traditional,
a natural, a wintry or a glitzy look,
the best trees on show are those
with trimmings made lovingly by
hand and kept for use year after year.

SELECTING TREES & CONTAINERS

WITH SO MANY CHRISTMAS TREES available, consumers are spoilt for choice – will you enjoy the evocative scent of a cut or potted fresh tree, the convenience of a realistic artificial tree, or something modern, stylish and completely different? The answer depends on your purposes; it helps to consider cost, space available and how long the tree needs to last. Once the tree is chosen, select a container to match.

BLUE SPRUCE
(See also page 19)
This prickly tree takes its name from its exceptional blue tinge which looks stunning with red and gold decorations. It retains its large needles quite well, but beware: they are painful to step on when fallen.

Small, glossy leaves

REAL TREES

Choose a potted tree with roots if you wish to replant it after Christmas. Alternatively, a cut tree can retain its needles quite well if placed in water.

Characteristic spiky, blue-green needles

BAY TREE (See also page 44)
This small leafy tree with a neat round shape is unusual, but ideal for a small room. Keep it in a pot, water it regularly and dress it with scaled-down decorations for Christmas. If you prefer, bays are available from garden centres clipped in the classic pine tree shape.

Variegated leaves add colour to the tree

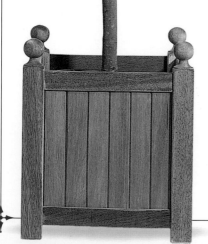

HOLLY TREE (See also page 28)
Instead of using just a few sprigs of festive holly, why not bring the whole tree indoors for Christmas? Choose a holly tree in glossy green with red berries, a cultivar on a long stem or an interesting variety with variegated leaves.

Pretty cane container hides a functional watertight pot

NORDMAN *(See also page 29)*
A soft and bushy Russian fir tree that tends to retain its glossy green needles, making it ideal to cut and keep indoors. The layered branches are easy to decorate.

SCOTS PINE *(See also page 33)*
This popular tree should retain its needles throughout the Christmas period. Take care when hanging glass baubles on the ends of the soft branches as they can easily slip off.

Containers

Place rooted trees in watertight containers filled with damp soil, and put cut trees in water, soil or sand.

Steel bucket practical for a real tree and easily filled with soil or water.

Decorated terracotta pot must be glazed if filled with damp soil.

Terracotta pot is ideal for all trees, and is inexpensive and easy to paint.

Copper bucket suits the colours of real trees rather than artificial ones.

NORWEGIAN SPRUCE *(See also page 45)*
Choose this green tree for its full and bushy shape, tapering to a single stem at the top. Needles are prickly and sparse, showing the bronze of the branches beneath.

Decorated wicker container hides a watertight pot

ARTIFICIAL TREES

A good quality artificial tree can be used for years.
If storage space is at a premium, opt for one that can
be dismantled. Styles are not limited to fir trees –
imaginative alternatives are available to suit all tastes.

TWIG TREE (*See also page 39*)
*Make a bold statement with a twig tree
which comes ready-assembled in a range
of sizes. Ideally suited to an earthy
look, the tree's twig branches make it
easy to decorate and the relatively
small size looks good in a window.*

Branches are easy to
coat with spray paint

Twiggy branches hold
decorations securely

Tree comes mounted on
suitable matching base

SILVER TWIG TREE
(*See also page 23*)
*Completely change the look of a
natural twig tree by spraying it with
silver paint – a glamorous base for
winter white festive decorations.*

Stands

**Can be adjusted to fit the trunk and are
ideal for trees that do not need watering.**

Dark green wrought iron stand
heavy enough to support a tree.

Red iron stand elegantly styled with
a wide base for extra stability.

Green tubular stand comes flat-packed
for convenient storage.

Each branch hooks into the trunk for easy assembly

Branches can be tweaked to produce the desired shape

METAL TREE (See also page 32)
An elegant metal tree is perfect for a modern, minimalist look which demands simple but well thought-out decorations. Leave it in position all year round and dress it up for Christmas.

Curled branches are ideal for hanging decorations

Shades of brown and green make branches look realistic

Pot made from strips of pine encircled by steel bands

ARTIFICIAL TREE
(See also pages 18, 22, 38)
A convincing artificial fir tree can be bent into a perfect shape and never drops its needles. Invest in a good one and it will last for years before beginning to look tired.

Gold-coloured metal with a matt finish

Wide base stops heavy tree from toppling over

TRADITIONAL TREES

REGAL RED AND GOLD are used to give these classic trees a traditional festive look, mixing old-fashioned and hand-made decorations with modern, shop-bought baubles. Wired bows, cranberry rings and salt dough shapes jostle for pride of place with glitzy gold tassels and garlands of ruby red beads, while wax candles add a timeless quality.

ANTIQUE LOOK

Smother an artificial tree with a thousand and one red and gold decorations, from heirlooms passed down the generations to new classic baubles with a twist. Lighting wax candles on the tree is not recommended so use white fairy lights for sparkle.

Cranberry ring shines among the baubles

Begin by winding white fairy lights around the tree

Garland of red beads spirals down the tree

Glossy glass balls fill in gaps

Position large velvet baubles where they will catch the light

Add tiny baskets of sweets on lower branches

Wine-red velvet cheat's bow (see page 105)

Red-painted terracotta pot adorned with a large bow and tassel

WE THREE KINGS

Choose a traditional crimson and gold theme to complement a beautiful blue spruce tree, using golden camels, opulent eastern crowns and sparkling strings of stars to tell the Christmas story. Finish with scarlet berries, thick shining tassels, gold snowflakes and iridescent baubles.

Bunch of holly berries

Weave a garland of gold stars among the branches

Gilded salt dough camel (see page 20)

Jewelled crown (see page 21)

Mirrored star

Scatter oversized tassels randomly on the branches

Terracotta pot contains damp soil to keep tree fresh

MAKING THE SALT DOUGH CAMELS

One quantity of dough will make about ten camels, but if you need fewer, unbaked dough will last for several weeks wrapped in clingfilm and kept in the refrigerator. Painting the shapes with a coat of varnish gives extra protection and shine.

◆ EQUIPMENT ◆

Pencil
Card
Scalpel
Cutting mat
Mixing bowl
Wooden spoon
Water
Flour, to dust
Rolling pin
Kitchen knife
Garlic press
Baking tray
Pin
Wire rack
Paintbrush
Varnish (optional)
Glue

Ingredients

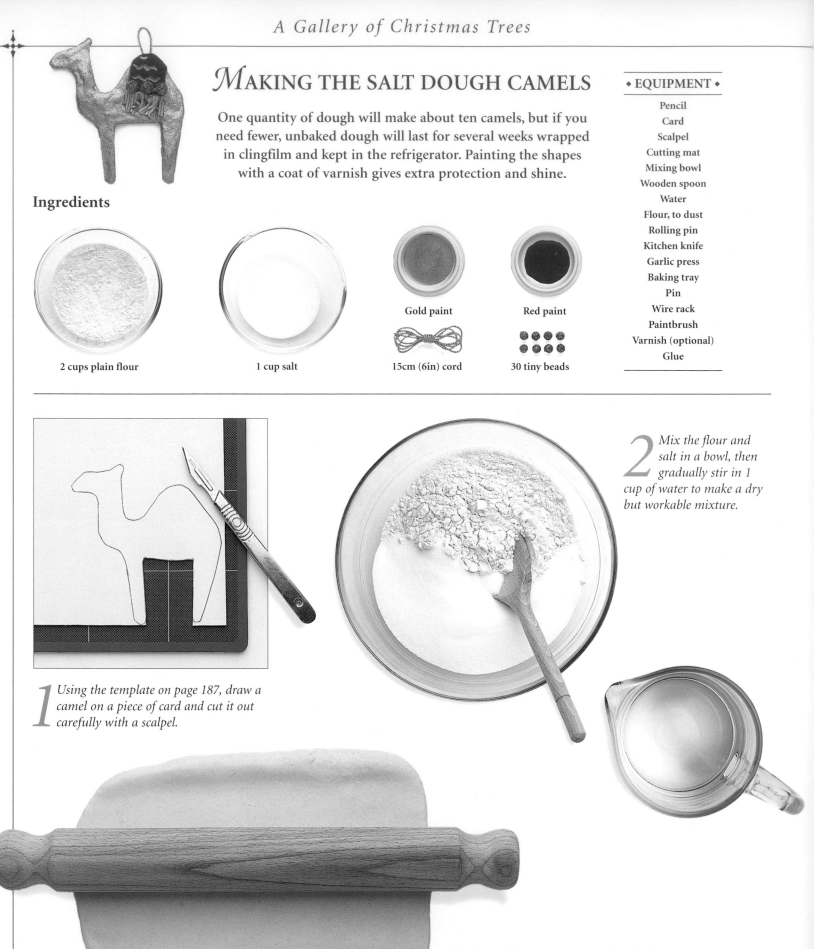

2 cups plain flour

1 cup salt

Gold paint

15cm (6in) cord

Red paint

30 tiny beads

1 Using the template on page 187, draw a camel on a piece of card and cut it out carefully with a scalpel.

2 Mix the flour and salt in a bowl, then gradually stir in 1 cup of water to make a dry but workable mixture.

3 Knead the mixture into a dough, place it on a floured surface and roll it out to about 6mm (¼in) thick.

4 Place the template on the dough and cut around it with a sharp knife. Repeat to make a total of ten camels.

5 Cut and engrave a little piece of dough to make a saddle for each camel, and push more dough through a garlic press to make a fringe for the saddle. Position these details on the camels ready for baking.

6 Place the camels on a baking tray and bake on the lowest setting for about 4 hours, or until the dough is hard but not brown. Prick the back of the camel with a pin to test for firmness. Cool on a wire rack.

7 When the camel has cooled, decorate it with red and gold paint. Varnish it if required – this will help to preserve the camel.

8 Loop a piece of gold cord and glue it to the back for hanging. Glue tiny beads to the saddle to finish.

Jewelled Crowns

Use the same method to make salt dough crowns that hang from the tree on loops of gold cord. Add intricate details, paint them red and gold and decorate with sparkly gold beads. Glue a loop of cord to the back to finish.

WHITE TREES

THESE GLITTERING TREES topped with silver stars sparkle like winter frost in the early morning sun. The delicate branches are laden with decorations made from frosted glass, translucent mother-of-pearl, masses of shimmering sequins, gleaming silver ribbon and shells wrapped in decadent lengths of pearlized beads. The effect is pure Christmas magic.

SNOW WHITE
Wind fairy lights and a shimmering silver ribbon in and out of the branches, working from the top down. Intersperse large white frosted baubles with lustred hearts, and add smaller silver balls in mirrored and etched glass to finish.

Artificial tree suits white and silver decorations

Use white fairy lights to highlight your favourite baubles

Large frosted bauble

Twist wire-edged silver ribbon around the tree

Terracotta pot sprayed silver and edged with a garland of silver beads

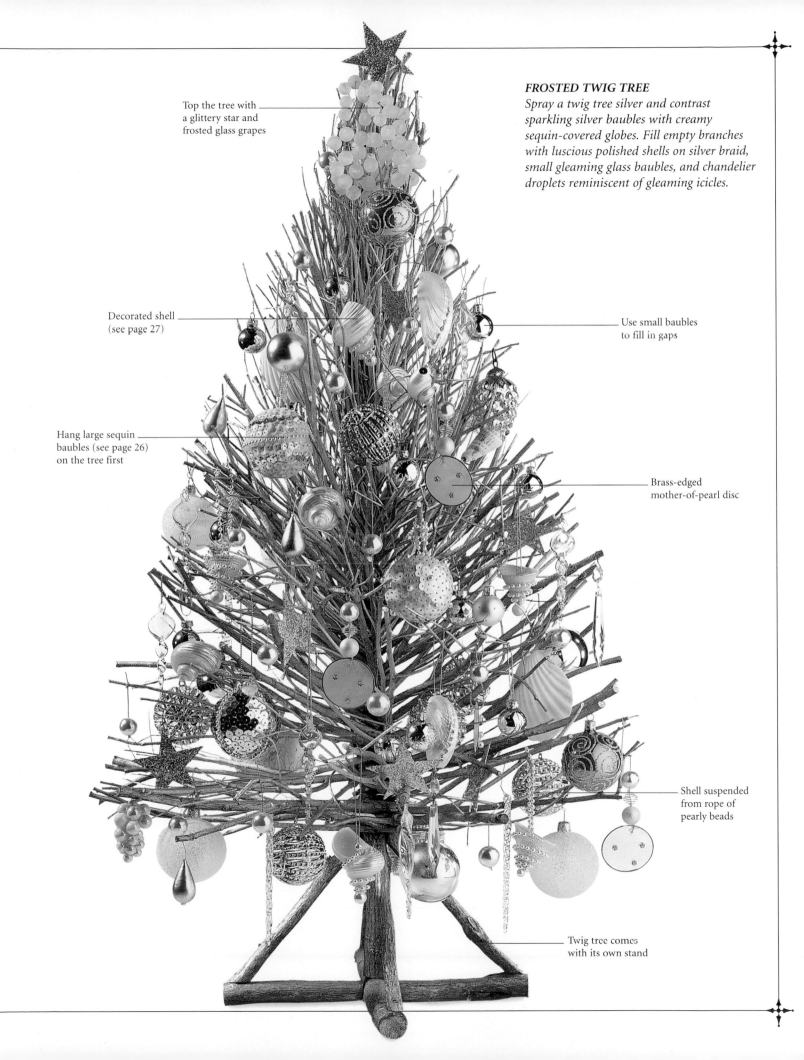

Top the tree with
a glittery star and
frosted glass grapes

FROSTED TWIG TREE
*Spray a twig tree silver and contrast
sparkling silver baubles with creamy
sequin-covered globes. Fill empty branches
with luscious polished shells on silver braid,
small gleaming glass baubles, and chandelier
droplets reminiscent of gleaming icicles.*

Decorated shell
(see page 27)

Use small baubles
to fill in gaps

Hang large sequin
baubles (see page 26)
on the tree first

Brass-edged
mother-of-pearl disc

Shell suspended
from rope of
pearly beads

Twig tree comes
with its own stand

PEARLY DECORATIONS

IN THE MONTHS BEFORE CHRISTMAS, start collecting sequins in shades of silver and cream, old pearl bead necklaces, fancy braid, shiny silver ribbons and highly polished seashells to turn into gleaming decorations. Buy cotton balls from craft shops and mix their round shapes with the elegance of long chandelier droplets for a stunning winter-white Christmas tree.

SEQUIN BAUBLE Ingredients

♦ EQUIPMENT ♦

Darning needle

Glue

Cotton ball, 20cm (8in) circumference

20cm (8in) bead trim

200 pearly sequins

50 silver sequins

250 pins

10cm (4in) silver cord

DECORATED SHELL Ingredients

7cm (2¾in) polished shell

20cm (8in) string pearl beads

2 small pearl beads

10cm (4in) silver cord

♦ EQUIPMENT ♦

Glue

Sequin bauble (see page 26)

String of beads used to suspend bauble

IRIDESCENT SEQUIN BAUBLE
Pin masses of gleaming sequins to a large cotton ball and add a smattering of round pearl beads to decorate.

Chandelier droplet hanging from decorated shell

Mirrored
bauble
reflects
the light

BAUBLE AND BOW
*Tie silver wire-edged
ribbon in a bow on
top of a small pearly
bauble decorated with
dots of glitter.*

Wire-edged
organza ribbon

Abalone shell
with natural
holes, from
a shell shop

Polished shell
wrapped with
beads (see page 27)

ICICLE DROPS
*Contrast an opaque patterned
glass bauble on silver braid
with graceful glass droplets.*

SHINING SHELLS
*Try shell shops for
shells polished until the
underlying mother-of-
pearl shows through.*

Silver sequin bauble
(see page 26)

MAKING THE SEQUIN BAUBLE

Stick to one or two simple colours of sequins, or experiment with alternating bands in vibrant colours. Wrapping strings of jazzy beads around the bauble adds glamour. WARNING: pinned sequin baubles can be dangerous for young children and animals.

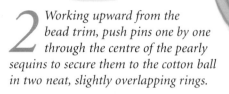

1 Glue the bead trim horizontally around the centre of the cotton ball, making sure the trim is straight.

2 Working upward from the bead trim, push pins one by one through the centre of the pearly sequins to secure them to the cotton ball in two neat, slightly overlapping rings.

4 Continue pinning on rings of pearl sequins until you reach the top of the ball, but do not cover the hole at the top. Repeat steps 2 to 4, working down from the bead trim.

3 After two rings of pearly sequins, add a row of silver sequins using the same technique.

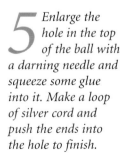

5 Enlarge the hole in the top of the ball with a darning needle and squeeze some glue into it. Make a loop of silver cord and push the ends into the hole to finish.

Pearls and Sequins

Studded Pearl Bauble
Cover a cotton ball completely with pearl sequins, then pin a few pearl beads on top of the sequins. Hang from a string of pearls.

Silver Sequin Bauble
Divide a cotton ball into quarters with four lines of pearl beads pinned in position, then fill the quarters with silver sequins.

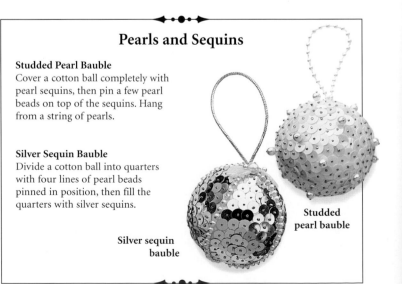

Silver sequin bauble

Studded pearl bauble

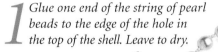

MAKING THE SHELL DECORATION

Choose shells that have been polished until the underlying mother-of-pearl shows through. Although ideally suited to spiral-shaped shells and strings of pearls, this simple method can be adapted for any type of shell or beads.

1 *Glue one end of the string of pearl beads to the edge of the hole in the top of the shell. Leave to dry.*

Join of cord and beads hidden by a small bead

2 *Wind the string of beads around the natural spiral of the shell, gluing it as you work. Cut the string when you reach the bottom.*

3 *Use strong glue to attach a small bead to the bottom of the shell so it covers the end of the string of beads. Leave to dry.*

4 *Fold the silver cord into a loop and glue it inside the top of the shell. Cover the join with a small bead.*

Decorated Shells

Limpet Shell
Use the same technique on a conical shell and suspend from a looped string of pearl beads.

Translucent Disc
Glue tiny silver stars to a brass-edged mother-of-pearl disc and attach to silver cord threaded with pearl beads and a silver spiral.

Abalone Shell
Suspend a glass droplet from a piece of cord threaded through the holes of an abalone shell.

Pearly Disc
Glue small pearly beads to a mother-of-pearl disc and thread on to silver cord.

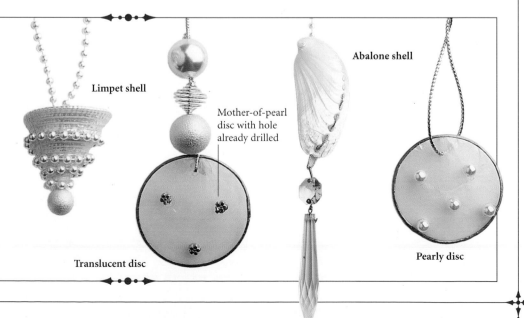

Limpet shell

Abalone shell

Mother-of-pearl disc with hole already drilled

Translucent disc

Pearly disc

COUNTRY-STYLE TREES

REJOICE IN ALL THINGS NATURAL at Christmas time, decking your tree out with flower petals, rich spices, ornate carved fruit, raffia baubles and rosebuds, all bathed in the natural glow of candlelight. For something completely different, suspend golden pears from a variegated holly tree, and perch a fat gold partridge in a raffia nest among the branches.

PARTRIDGE IN A PEAR TREE
For a quirky take on the well-known Christmas carol, perch a golden partridge in a red raffia nest among the branches of a traditional holly tree. Golden pears hanging from the lowest branches complete the look.

Chicken wire scrunched into shape and sprayed gold

Variegated holly, clipped into shape

Card pear covered in gold leaf

FRUIT, SPICE AND ALL THINGS NICE

Fill the room with scent by gluing aromatic spices, such as star anise, and small chillies to cotton balls, and by using dried oranges, rose petals and bunches of oregano as decorations. Echo the deep green of a Nordman tree with soft green candles and complete the earthy theme with a woven cane pot.

Wooden animal shape covered in a light dusting of chalk

Green wax candles for decoration

Dried orange bauble (see page 31)

String bauble echoes the natural theme

Flower ball (see page 30)

MAKING THE FLOWER BALL

Dried roses are ideal for making flower balls as the petals are slightly flexible, quite flat and retain much of their colour when dried. Carefully open the petals out and glue them so the best side faces outward.

Ingredients

10 dried roses per ball

Cotton ball, 20cm (8in) circumference

Stub wire (medium gauge)

◆ EQUIPMENT ◆

Darning needle

Glue

Slightly overlap each ring of petals to hide the yellow tops

1 Gently pull the petals from the roses, making sure they are not damaged in the process. Discard imperfect petals.

2 Starting at the bottom of the ball, glue the petals on one by one so they form a slightly overlapping ring.

3 Continue gluing the petals on, working around the ball toward the top, creating neat rings of petals.

4 When the ball is completely covered, use a darning needle to enlarge the hole in the top. Fill it with glue and push in a piece of stub wire. To finish, bend the wire into a hook for hanging.

Spicy Balls

Use the same technique to make baubles covered with tiny dried chillies, aduki beans or dried star anise, which fills the room with a lovely aniseed scent. Wash your hands after handling dried chillies.

Dried chillies

Aduki beans

Dried star anise

MAKING THE CITRUS BAUBLES

The thick skin of oranges lends itself well to carving, so practise on them before attempting the thinner skin of limes. For perfectly dried baubles choose very fresh, unwaxed produce and leave somewhere warm and dry for about two weeks.

Ingredients

Fresh, unwaxed citrus fruit

Stub wires (thick gauge)

1 Use a canelle knife to start carving a spiral pattern into the skin of a plump, round, unwaxed orange.

2 Slowly continue the spiral until it reaches the bottom of the orange. If the peel breaks, start again from that point. Carve different patterns into other fruit (see inset) to make an entire set.

Ready to dry   **Dried**

3 Leave the fruit somewhere warm to dry for about two weeks. Any dampness in the atmosphere will ruin the baubles.

4 Make a hole in the top of the orange with a needle, glue a stub wire in the hole and bend into a hook to finish.

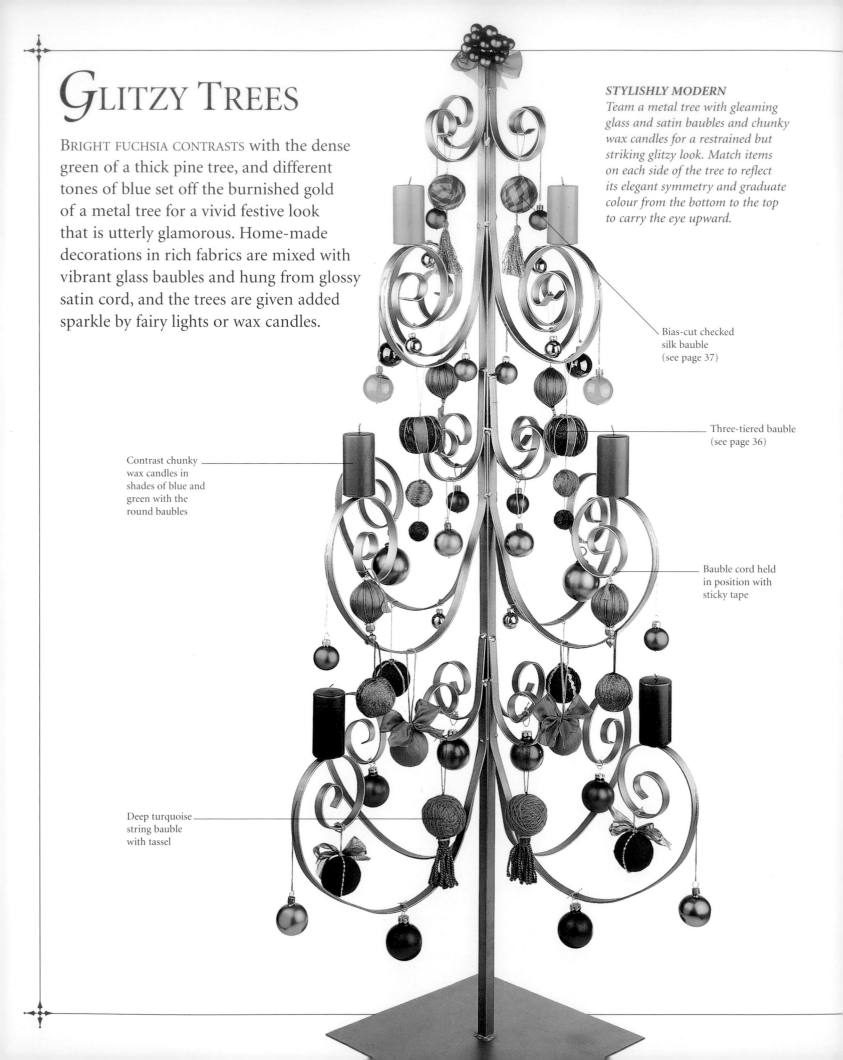

GLITZY TREES

BRIGHT FUCHSIA CONTRASTS with the dense green of a thick pine tree, and different tones of blue set off the burnished gold of a metal tree for a vivid festive look that is utterly glamorous. Home-made decorations in rich fabrics are mixed with vibrant glass baubles and hung from glossy satin cord, and the trees are given added sparkle by fairy lights or wax candles.

STYLISHLY MODERN
Team a metal tree with gleaming glass and satin baubles and chunky wax candles for a restrained but striking glitzy look. Match items on each side of the tree to reflect its elegant symmetry and graduate colour from the bottom to the top to carry the eye upward.

Bias-cut checked silk bauble (see page 37)

Three-tiered bauble (see page 36)

Contrast chunky wax candles in shades of blue and green with the round baubles

Bauble cord held in position with sticky tape

Deep turquoise string bauble with tassel

PINK, PURPLE AND GOLD

Load a Scots pine tree with dazzling coloured glass baubles, raw silk pouches, shiny foil crackers and tiny wrapped gifts nestling in the branches. Scatter golden garlands throughout, add multi-coloured fairy lights and place a theatrical star on top to steal the limelight.

Fairy light shines on the gold star

Shiny silk string baubles dotted randomly on tree

Tiny gift wrapped in lustrous paper

Rest tiny foil crackers on the bushy branches

Pouch made from luxurious silk saturated in colour

Tree stands in damp soil in a plastic pot, disguised with a layer of moss and a blue cane container

Mauve-blue cane pot tied with cerise ribbon

FABRIC BAUBLES

WIND SHIMMERING FABRICS AND TRIMMINGS in jewel-like colours around lightweight cotton balls to make sumptuous tree decorations and add textural contrast to the extravagant display with shop-bought glass and spangled baubles. Break up their strong outlines with iridescent ribbons twisted into bows, and suspend your opulent creations from lengths of coloured tinsel ribbon, glittering braid, silk yarn and gold cord.

THREE-TIERED BAUBLE Ingredients

Cotton ball, 20cm (8in) circumference

Cotton ball, 10cm (4in) circumference

5m (5½yd) knitting yarn

Three coloured knitting yarns, 8m (8½yd) each

Cotton ball, 8cm (3in) circumference

◆ EQUIPMENT ◆

Tweezers

Darning needle

Fabric glue

50cm (½yd) thick gold rope

3m (3¼yd) thin twisted gold cord

5m (5½yd) knitting yarn

CHECKED SILK BAUBLE Ingredients

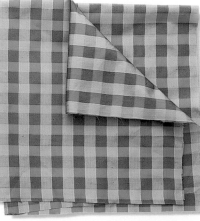

50cm (20in) gold cord

◆ EQUIPMENT ◆

Dressmaking pins

Fabric scissors

Iron

Fabric glue

Silk, 50 x 50cm (20 x 20in)

Gimp pin

Cotton ball, 20cm (8in) circumference

Shop-bought gold tassel

GOLD GLITTER BALL
Soften the effect of a shop-bought gold bauble with a delicate gold and turquoise voile bow.

Glittering theatrical tassel

CHECKED SILK BAUBLE
Wrap thin strips of gleaming checked silk haphazardly around a ball for a rich, vibrant effect. An over-sized gold tassel provides a bold splash of glitter.

GLASS BAUBLES
Combine metallic glass baubles with fabric decorations.

JADE BALL
Set jade dupion silk against an elegant green voile bow.

Sparking gold cord connects each ball

THREE-TIERED BAUBLE
Wrap silky turquoise, purple and multi-coloured yarns around three balls. Use gold cord to highlight the coloured segments and lead the eye through the decoration.

PLUM BALL
Wind vivid purple yarn on to a ball and enhance it with a wire-edged bow and gold braid.

GREEN AND PURPLE BAUBLE
Thread emerald green and deep purple knitting yarns through a cotton ball to create solid blocks of colour edged with gold ric-rac braid. Secure blue tinsel ribbon to the bauble with a gimp pin.

MAKING THE THREE-TIERED BAUBLE

First make a hole in the large cotton ball (see inset below). Then divide each of the three 8m (8½yd) lengths of yarn into quarters before threading them through the hole. Yarns are wound on to the small balls and glued.

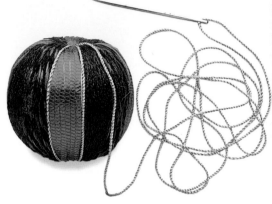

1 Thread one piece of turquoise yarn on to a needle, pass it through the hole in the large ball and tie it to form a loop.

2 Twist the knot into the hole to conceal it and continue threading the yarn through the ball, as shown, creating a segment of colour. Secure the end by hooking it under previous turns of yarn.

3 Repeat with one piece of purple yarn, then one piece of multi-coloured yarn. Alternate the colours until the ball is covered. Then thread 2.75m (3yd) of thin gold cord around each segment. Secure as before.

4 Wind a length of purple yarn around the small ball and a length of turquoise yarn around the medium ball.

Secure the loose end of yarn with glue

5 With a darning needle, pull the rest of the gold cord through the smaller balls, knotting it as you go and leaving 2.5cm (1in) of cord between each ball. Glue the cord into the hole at the bottom of the large ball.

Leave 2.5cm (1in) of gold cord between each ball

Dab glue in the top of the hole

Enlarging the hole in a ball

Using tweezers, gently pull out the paper-like wadding from the tiny hole in a cotton ball, gradually increasing the width of the hole. Then work from the other end of the ball in the same way until the hole is about 2.5cm (1in) wide all through the ball.

6 Glue a 6cm (2½in) piece of gold rope around the top of the hole in the large ball. Knot one end of the remaining rope and glue it into the hole. Tie the other end of the rope to the tree.

MAKING THE CHECKED SILK BAUBLE

Start by cutting the silk on the bias (see inset steps below) to create thin strips that mould themselves easily around the circular cotton shape. The number of strips you use depends on how you wrap them on to the ball.

Cutting strips on the bias

1 Fold the square of silk diagonally in half to locate the longest bias line. Place pins along this folded edge at 1cm (½in) intervals.

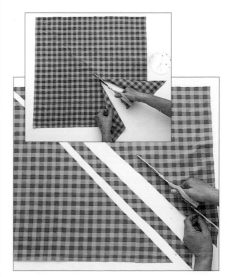

2 Open up the square and cut along the bias, removing the pins as you go. Continue to cut each half of silk into 3.5cm (1½in) wide strips.

3 Turn the raw edges of the strips over and pin to the wrong side of the silk. Press them with an iron, removing the pins, to create a neat finish.

Wrap the second strip across the first

1 *Wrap the longest strip of silk around the ball, securing the end by overlapping it with the next turn of fabric.*

2 *Wind the next longest strip on to the ball so that it crosses the first. Keep adding strips until the ball is covered.*

Push the gimp pin through the end of silk

3 *Secure the last strip with a gimp pin. Hook a loop of gold cord with knotted ends under the pin for hanging.*

4 *Push a pin through the top of the tassel, dab glue on the pinhead, and push it into the bottom of the ball.*

EDIBLE TREES

A CHRISTMAS TREE CREAKING under the weight of delicious-looking edible decorations is a delight to the eye as well as the palate. Choose a natural colour scheme using biscuits and dried fruit, or pander to the children of the house with a tempting mix of coloured sweeties, lollipops, wrapped chocolates and net bags of gold-wrapped chocolate coins.

CONFECTIONERY DELIGHT
For a tree that is guaranteed a hit with children, tie cotton thread around the ends of wrapped sweets to make long garlands, and bundle small sweets into squares of cellophane tied with colourful cord. Attach brightly wrapped sweets and lollies to the branches with lengths of cotton and set the whole tree ablaze with red fairy lights.

Candy cane hooked over branch

Coloured sweeties in cellophane packets

Tie wrapped chocolates to a long piece of thread to make a garland

Quirky vegetable-shaped baubles

Tie long pieces of marshmallow to the tree with ribbon

Sacks of gold coins placed randomly

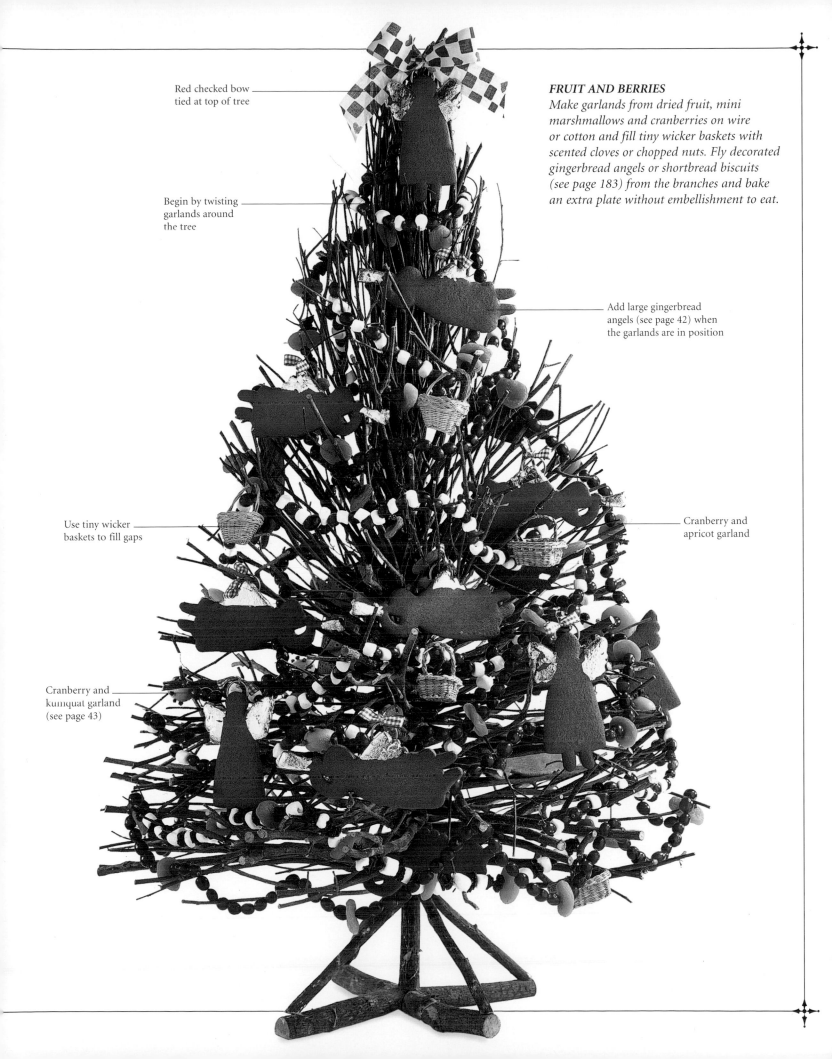

Red checked bow
tied at top of tree

Begin by twisting
garlands around
the tree

Use tiny wicker
baskets to fill gaps

Cranberry and
kumquat garland
(see page 43)

FRUIT AND BERRIES
Make garlands from dried fruit, mini marshmallows and cranberries on wire or cotton and fill tiny wicker baskets with scented cloves or chopped nuts. Fly decorated gingerbread angels or shortbread biscuits (see page 183) from the branches and bake an extra plate without embellishment to eat.

Add large gingerbread
angels (see page 42) when
the garlands are in position

Cranberry and
apricot garland

EDIBLE TREE DECORATIONS

FOR DECORATIVE FESTIVE garlands, thread shiny cranberries and kumquats studded with aromatic cloves on to a reel of wire, or alternate dried cherries, apricot slices and mini marshmallows. Suspend gingerbread angels with golden wings from gold rings trimmed with ribbon, and bake an unadorned batch for eating (one quantity makes ten angels).

GINGERBREAD ANGEL Ingredients

SAFETY FIRST
Do not eat angels with rings glued to them; bake a separate plate for eating.

1 quantity gingerbread dough (see page 181)

Pad of gold leaf (optional)

White of egg, optional

10 curtain rings

150cm (59in) gold thread

1m (1yd) checked ribbon

◆ EQUIPMENT ◆

Thin card	Wire rack
Pencil	Bowl (optional)
Scissors	
Flour, to dust	Egg whisk (optional)
Rolling pin	
Kitchen knife	Fine paintbrush (optional)
Non-stick baking parchment	Spoon
Baking tray	Glue

CRANBERRY GARLAND Ingredients

5 kumquats

50 cloves

◆ EQUIPMENT ◆

Wire cutters

70 cranberries per 1m (1yd) wire

Reel of wire (medium gauge)

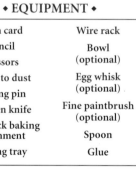

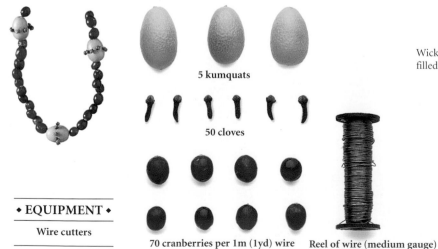

Wicker basket filled with cloves

NATURAL COLOURS
Give decorations a natural feel using the muted colours of dried fruit, cloves, wicker baskets, gingerbread and gingham ribbon, and brighten the effect with fresh kumquats.

Cranberries and marshmallows strung in a garland

Marshmallows, threaded with alternate dried apricot slices and dried cherries

Cranberries and dried apricot slices

Cranberry garland adorned with kumquats (see page 43)

Flying angel (see page 188 for template)

MAKING THE GINGERBREAD ANGELS

For ten angels, make up one quantity of gingerbread dough following steps 1 and 2 of the Gingerbread House recipe on page 181. If you do not wish to use gold leaf, try using coloured icing or gold paste from a cake-decorating shop.

1 Copy the angel template on page 188 on to thin card and cut it out. Mix the gingerbread dough and roll it out on a lightly floured surface to a thickness of about 6mm (¼in).

Re-roll the dough to get ten neat angels

2 Place the card angel on the dough and cut around it with a small kitchen knife. Repeat to make ten angels.

3 Line a baking tray with non-stick baking parchment and place the gingerbread angels carefully on it. Bake at 190°C/375°F/gas 5 for 8-10 minutes, until firm. Cool on a wire rack.

4 If using gold leaf, lightly whisk the white of an egg and paint it on to the angel's wings with a fine paintbrush. Otherwise decorate the angel as desired and add the ring and bow as directed in step 6.

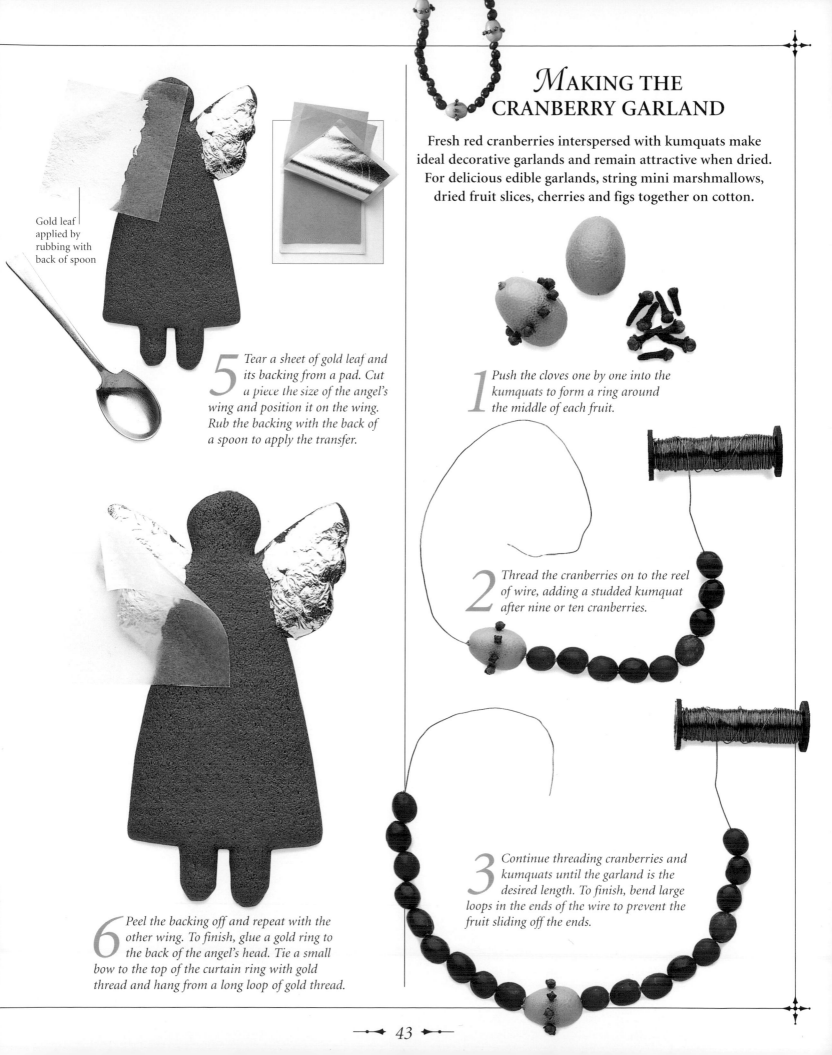

Gold leaf applied by rubbing with back of spoon

5 *Tear a sheet of gold leaf and its backing from a pad. Cut a piece the size of the angel's wing and position it on the wing. Rub the backing with the back of a spoon to apply the transfer.*

6 *Peel the backing off and repeat with the other wing. To finish, glue a gold ring to the back of the angel's head. Tie a small bow to the top of the curtain ring with gold thread and hang from a long loop of gold thread.*

MAKING THE CRANBERRY GARLAND

Fresh red cranberries interspersed with kumquats make ideal decorative garlands and remain attractive when dried. For delicious edible garlands, string mini marshmallows, dried fruit slices, cherries and figs together on cotton.

1 *Push the cloves one by one into the kumquats to form a ring around the middle of each fruit.*

2 *Thread the cranberries on to the reel of wire, adding a studded kumquat after nine or ten cranberries.*

3 *Continue threading cranberries and kumquats until the garland is the desired length. To finish, bend large loops in the ends of the wire to prevent the fruit sliding off the ends.*

CARNIVAL TREES

HOT, RIOTOUS COLOURS bring instant warmth and sunshine indoors for Christmas. Golden suns, vibrant tinplate shapes, dazzling baubles and long garlands of paper beads almost hide the branches of a Norwegian tree, and vividly coloured mini citrus fruit nestle among the glossy green leaves of a bay tree.

TIE A YELLOW RIBBON
Wire tiny citrus-coloured bows to kumquats and limequats and scatter them evenly throughout the leaves of a bushy bay tree. Match the bows with a lemon yellow ribbon spiralled around the trunk.

Cheat's bow (see page 105) attached to limequat and fixed to branch with wire

Thick yellow ribbon wound around trunk

FESTIVE FUN

Crowd a Norwegian tree with masses of paper, tin and glass decorations in the craziest colours possible. Fill spaces with jazzy baubles, snake a garland of paper beads through the branches, and add multi-coloured fairy lights to finish.

Tinplate fish
(see page 46)

Aztec-style sun

Multi-coloured
paper bead garland
(see page 47)

MAKING THE TINPLATE FISH

Check your telephone directory for suppliers of sheets of tinplate and choose a thinnish sheet which is easy to cut. To avoid damaging the table top when punching patterns into tinplate, use a piece of soft, thick card as a base.

♦ EQUIPMENT ♦

Sharp pencil

Card

Scalpel or craft knife

Cutting mat

Old scissors

Thick card

Nail

Hammer

Hole punch

Ingredients

Tinplate, 16 x 6cm (6½ x 2½in)

Cellulose marker pens

15cm (6in) cord

1 Copy the fish template on page 186 on to a piece of card and cut it out carefully with a scalpel.

2 Place the card template on the sheet of tinplate and score around it with a sharp pencil.

3 Use old, blunt scissors to cut carefully around the scored line, making sure there are no jagged edges.

Tap the nail gently to avoid piercing the tin

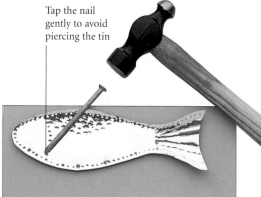

4 Place the tinplate fish on a piece of thick card and use a nail and hammer to punch a pattern on the shiny side.

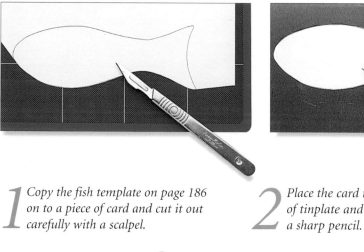

5 Use coloured cellulose marker pens to decorate the shiny side of the fish. Pierce one end with a hole punch and thread a piece of cord through it to hang (see inset).

MAKING THE PAPER BEAD GARLAND

Start amassing pieces of scrap paper: most types can be used
to make these beads as long as they are brightly coloured.
Thick sugar paper makes heavy, bulky beads, and thinner
paper produces more refined and delicate beads.

Ingredients

Selection of coloured papers,
45 x 35cm (18 x 13¾in)

1.8m (2yd)
coloured cord

♦ EQUIPMENT ♦

PVA glue

Paintbrush

3 garden canes,
50cm (20in) long

Sharp knife

*1 Brush PVA glue on to the
reverse of one piece of
coloured paper, leaving
about 7.5cm (3in) at the
bottom without any glue.*

*2 Lay the cane across the end of the
unpasted section of paper and roll
the paper tightly around it. When
you reach the end of the paper leave the
cane in place while the glue dries to
prevent warping. Repeat with the
other sheets of coloured paper.*

*3 When the glue is dry, use a sharp
knife to slice the paper tube into
2.5cm (1in) beads. Leave the cane in
place while slicing to prevent the beads being
squashed in the process.*

*4 Measure out a piece of cord as long as
you want the garland to be. Thread
the beads on to it one by one, tying the
string in a loop around the bead at each end
of the garland to secure.*

WREATHS, GARLANDS & FLOWERS

Glossy evergreen leaves and colourful berries have always symbolized the hope of new life in the depths of a northern winter. Use them in combination with fresh or dried flowers, fruit and nuts to make seasonal wreaths, garlands and door swags that will transform your home into a welcoming venue for Christmas celebrations.

CHRISTMAS WREATHS

NEUTRAL MUTED COLOURS highlighted with shimmery hints of gold and bronze make a perfect palette for inspiringly different Christmas wreaths. Focus on texture, contrasting the natural roughness of reindeer moss, bark and barley with smooth satin and soft wispy ribbons tied in luxurious bows, then crown the festive look with a bunch of sparkly berries.

Berries still
look good
when dried

RUSTIC BARK
*Wrap a ribbon around a
shop-bought bark wreath
and tie in a bow at the top. Glue
a bunch of dried yellow rosebuds
under the bow and tie gold-painted
wooden hearts to the ribbon.*

Gold mesh
ribbon

DRIED BERRIES
*Wire clusters of fresh pyracantha
berries to a strong wire frame and
tie a gauzy ribbon in a bow at the
top. Leave the berries to dry.*

PALE AND INTERESTING
*Decorate a shop-bought reindeer
moss wreath with a bunch of gold
artificial berries and two voile
ribbons in toning colours.*

COUNTRY STYLE
*Glue a bunch of pyracantha berries
and a wired rosette of ribbon to a
small twisted barley wreath.*

BRONZED IVY
*Wrap long strands of ivy around a square
piece of wire and spray with copper paint.
Glue on a bronze satin ribbon tied in a
flat bow.*

CHILLI RING
*Thread dried chillies on to a
wire and bend into shape. Glue
together rosettes of wire-edged
ribbon and raffia and wire
them in position at the top.*

Dried chillies packed
on to an oval of wire

NUTS AND SEEDS
*Glue whole nuts, seed pods, seeds and
spices randomly on to a shop-bought
wreath base and highlight some of them
with gilt creme. Finish with a wire-edged
taffeta bow positioned on one side.*

Bundle of
cinnamon
sticks

FESTIVE GREEN WREATH

AN EXTRAVAGANT WREATH on the front door gives guests a hint of the seasonal festivities to be enjoyed inside the house, and this unusual wreath is large enough to adorn any outside door. Be a little different with a home-made diamond-shaped base, and use an eye-catching mix of fresh and dried leaves, flowers and fruit, brightened for Christmas with shiny baubles in shades of blue and green. To finish, draw the eye to the centre with two lavish bauble-trimmed bows made from thick green ribbons edged in gold.

FESTIVE GREEN WREATH Ingredients

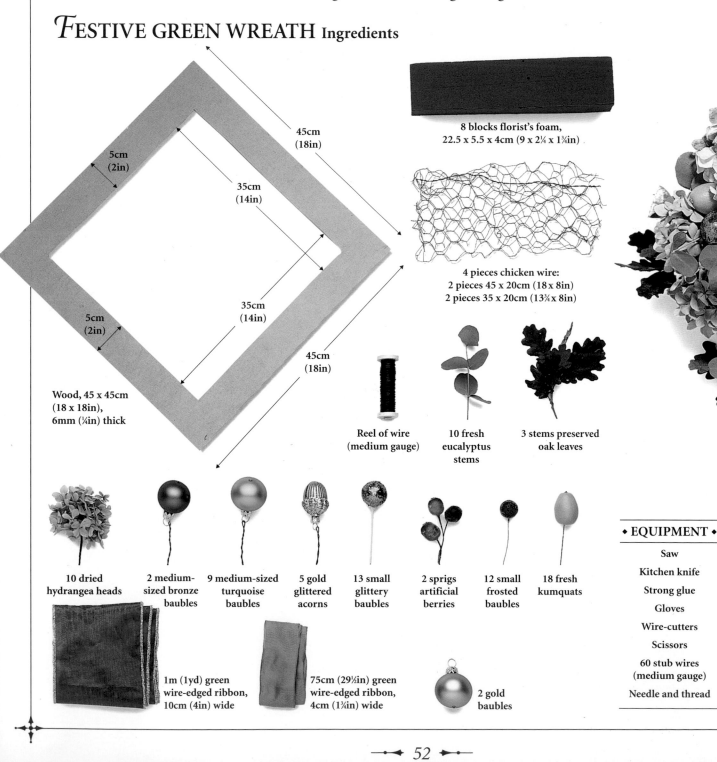

45cm (18in)

5cm (2in)

35cm (14in)

35cm (14in)

5cm (2in)

45cm (18in)

Wood, 45 x 45cm (18 x 18in), 6mm (¼in) thick

8 blocks florist's foam, 22.5 x 5.5 x 4cm (9 x 2¼ x 1⅜in)

4 pieces chicken wire: 2 pieces 45 x 20cm (18 x 8in) 2 pieces 35 x 20cm (13¾ x 8in)

Reel of wire (medium gauge)

10 fresh eucalyptus stems

3 stems preserved oak leaves

10 dried hydrangea heads

2 medium-sized bronze baubles

9 medium-sized turquoise baubles

5 gold glittered acorns

13 small glittery baubles

2 sprigs artificial berries

12 small frosted baubles

18 fresh kumquats

1m (1yd) green wire-edged ribbon, 10cm (4in) wide

75cm (29½in) green wire-edged ribbon, 4cm (1¼in) wide

2 gold baubles

◆ EQUIPMENT ◆

Saw

Kitchen knife

Strong glue

Gloves

Wire-cutters

Scissors

60 stub wires (medium gauge)

Needle and thread

Fresh kumquats
add colour

Small pieces
of hydrangea
fill in gaps

MAKING THE WREATH

Before you start, break the hydrangea heads, eucalyptus and oak leaves into small sprigs and cut natural stems quite short. Slip pieces of stub wire into kumquats and twist it through the top of the baubles so they can be easily secured in the foam.

Chicken wire covers florist's foam completely and wraps around to the back

Blocks of florist's foam cut to fit frame

1 *Cut a 35cm (14in) square from the wood to leave a 5cm (2in) frame. Place the blocks of florist's foam on top of the wooden frame, cutting them to size so they cover it entirely, as shown. Glue the florist's foam in position.*

2 *Wearing gloves to protect your hands, bend the pieces of chicken wire around the frame and bind by wrapping the reel of wire around it. Make a wire loop for hanging and attach it to the back of the frame in the top corner (see inset).*

Leaves pushed in at different angles to give a natural look

Eucalyptus and oak leaves broken down into small sprigs

3 *Push sprigs of eucalyptus and oak leaves into the florist's foam, covering both the top and sides of the frame.*

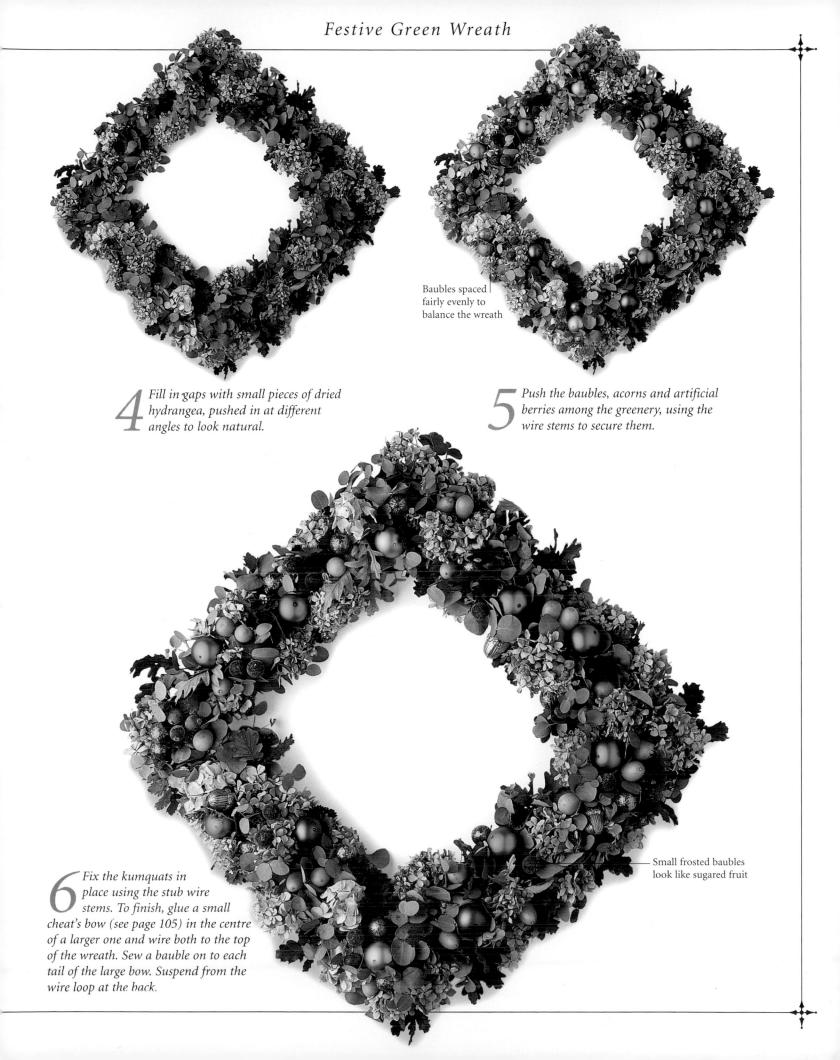

4 Fill in gaps with small pieces of dried hydrangea, pushed in at different angles to look natural.

5 Push the baubles, acorns and artificial berries among the greenery, using the wire stems to secure them.

Baubles spaced fairly evenly to balance the wreath

Small frosted baubles look like sugared fruit

6 Fix the kumquats in place using the stub wire stems. To finish, glue a small cheat's bow (see page 105) in the centre of a larger one and wire both to the top of the wreath. Sew a bauble on to each tail of the large bow. Suspend from the wire loop at the back.

DOOR SWAGS

A DOOR SWAG MAKES a stylish alternative to the traditional Christmas wreath, brightening up the house with festive glamour. For the front door, make a robust evergreen swag that will withstand harsh weather, and use dried flowers, scented spices and pretty ribbons to make more delicate arrangements for doors inside the home.

BEECH TWIGS
Tie beech twigs in a bunch with wire and overtie with a red raffia bow. Wire tiny limequats and raffia bows on to the branches and finish with a stuffed tree decoration.

EVERGREEN DROP
Starting at the bottom, wire bunches of blue spruce to a cane so that each layer slightly overlaps the one below. Add red glass grapes at the joins and tie two taffeta cheat's bows (see page 105) at the top.

FLORAL CORNET
Remove the leaves from a bunch of celosia and place it in a cone of chicken wire lined with damp moss. Squeeze it to secure the flowers, then cover by pinning on overlapping celosia leaves. Decorate with a spiral of gold braid and hang from a loop of ribbon.

Celosia leaves pinned in place with fine wire

Top edge of celosia leaves neatly folded over

HOLLY AND IVY BUNCH
Make a flat bundle of blue spruce, holly and ivy and wire it at the top, overtying with a green taffeta ribbon. Decorate with cranberries threaded on to rings of wire.

Miniature wreath made of cranberries

DRIED SWAG
Adorn the front of a shop-bought twig and spruce swag with cinnamon sticks, dried hydrangea, an artichoke sprayed gold and artificial apples. Wire or glue the items in place and finish with a glossy double bow (see page 105).

GARLANDS

BRING THE DELIGHTS of the garden indoors for festive celebrations by making a bountiful Christmas garland for the house. Create a garland with drop swags to fit around a doorway or window arch, lay a long garland down the centre of the dining table or entwine it around stair banisters for sheer flamboyance.

Sparkling artificial berries wired to the centre of bows

Double bows in contrasting russet and gold ribbons

GILDED GARLAND
Cover a shop-bought drop swag garland of overlapping bay leaves with gilding creme and twist a russet rope around the main section. Decorate the swags with double bows made using contrasting wire-edged ribbons (see page 105).

Pecans wired to the rope

Shop-bought
bark apples

FESTIVE FIR SWAG
*Decorate an artificial fir swag by wiring to
it gold-sprayed dried fruit, nuts and seeds,
apples made from tree bark, artificial cones,
nuts and berries. Finish with bows made
from wire-edged ribbon (see page 105).*

SPRUCE AND SPICE
*Wire sprigs of blue spruce on to
a thick rope that is easy to drape
around furniture. Cover it with
wired pecans, cones, dried chillies
and orange slices, and bunches of
twigs and cinnamon sticks.*

FRUIT GARLAND

PACK A LUSCIOUS GARLAND with festive evergreens, fresh red apples, carved dried citrus fruit (see page 31), dried pomegranates and wired pecans, and add sophistication with shimmering wire-edged ribbons in gold-green and burgundy.

FRUIT GARLAND Ingredients

110cm (43in)

Twig frame

45cm (18in)

Drop swags

Chicken wire, 150 x 20cm (59 x 8in)

Small bag of fresh moss

Reel of fine wire

8 bamboo sticks, 25cm (10in)

Fresh red apples add colour and shine

20 sprigs
sarcococca

15 sprigs
yew

80 sprigs
berried ivy

30 strands
ivy

15 sprigs
variegated holly

45 sprigs
Senecio greyii

◆ EQUIPMENT ◆

Gloves

Wire-cutters

4 stub wires
(medium gauge)

21 wired
pecans

9 carved, dried
citrus fruit
(see page 31)

4 dried
pomegranates

11 red
apples

2.5m (2¾ yd) gold
wire-edged ribbon
1.8m (2yd) burgundy
wire-edged ribbon

Dried lime with carved
skin (see page 31)

Long-tailed
double bow
made with
ribbon and
stub wire

MAKING THE GARLAND

The garland is simple to make using a ready-made twig frame
with detachable drop swags. Buy pecans ready-wired and
push lengths of bamboo stick into dried citrus fruit,
pomegranates and apples as you work to secure.

*1 Place handfuls of moss
on to the main section of the twig frame,
wrapping the reel of wire around it as you
go to hold it in place. There is no need to cover
the back of the garland.*

*2 Wearing gloves, wrap chicken wire
around the frame, over the moss, and
wind more wire around it to secure.*

Loop attaches swags
to main part and is
used for hanging the
garland when finished

*3 Cover the drop swags
in moss secured with the
reel of wire (see step 1).
Attach the swags to the main
section using the loops provided.*

Sprigs pushed in
randomly to give
a natural effect

*4 Push the sprigs of
sarcococca, yew and
berried ivy into all
sections of the frame, hooking
the stems into the wire.*

5 Push in the strands of ivy, variegated holly and *Senecio greyii* randomly, making sure the chicken wire is completely covered.

6 Fill in any gaps on the main section of the garland with the pecans, dried citrus fruit and pomegranates, securing with lengths of bamboo stick pushed into the fruit and the frame.

Dried fruit secured with bamboo stick

Use the loops at the back to hang the garland

7 Push lengths of bamboo stick into the apples and position them along the main section. Finally, make four double bows in ribbons of contrasting colours (see page 105). Position two at each end, with a long curl of excess ribbon down each swag.

TOPIARY TREES

COLLECT A CLUSTER of miniature topiary trees in varying shapes and colours for an original Christmas display. A tiny conical evergreen topped with a majestic purple bauble mimics a Christmas tree, while a larger ball of holly and berried ivy sits on top of deliciously scented cinnamon sticks. Dried hydrangea heads, gold balls and pink paper flowers make a lasting arrangement that contrasts well with the glossy density of evergreens.

MAKING A TOPIARY TREE

Ingredients

Block florist's foam,
34 x 10 x 8cm
(13½ x 4 x 3¼in)

Pot, 14cm
(5½in) tall

25cm (10in)
bamboo stick

4 branches
box

Small
bauble

◆ EQUIPMENT ◆

Kitchen knife

1 stub wire
(medium gauge)

Flat square surface
for bauble at top
of pyramid

Box sprigs
pushed together
to hide foam

1 *Cut a block of florist's
foam into two pieces,
each 10 x 10 x 8cm
(4 x 4 x 3¼in). Place one on
top of the other and push the
bamboo stick through both of
them. Use a kitchen knife to
cut the foam into a four-sided
pyramid, leaving a small flat
surface at the top.*

2 *Cut the remaining foam to fit the pot
and put it inside. Sit the pyramid on
top, using the bamboo stick to secure.*

3 *Break the branches of
box into tiny sprigs and,
starting at the bottom,
push them one by one into the
foam pyramid so no foam shows.*

4 *Gradually build up
the box sprigs until
the foam is completely
covered. To finish, slip a wire through
the loop on the bauble and push it into
the flat surface of foam at the top.*

HOLLY AND IVY SPHERE

Stand a bunch of long cinnamon sticks in a pot filled with dry florist's foam and push a ball of damp florist's foam covered in sprigs of holly and berried ivy on to the cinnamon sticks. Cover the filled pot with a layer of velvety bun moss and decorate with a gold star and a scattering of tiny gifts.

PRETTY IN PINK

Push dried hydrangea heads, paper roses and gold papier-mâché balls on wires into dry florist's foam and wedge it into a pot. Finish with a lavish bow.

Cinnamon sticks act as a stem

MINI TREE

Contrast shiny evergreen leaves with purple and matt gold for a regal look.

FESTIVE FLOWERS

FOR A FRESH TAKE ON Christmas decorations, try an eye-catching arrangement of flowers in traditional festive colours.
Keep each arrangement simple in itself and, for maximum impact, group it with others that are different in height, size, colour and texture. Clever use of plain glass vases in interesting shapes allows the flowers to take centre stage.

Classic display of red short-stemmed roses

Dense grouping of ranunculus, gerbera, red anemones and poinsettia

White anemones cut down short to fit a small square tank

Fleshy stems of red
hippeastrum stand
tall in a vase

Masses of juicy red
berries contrast
with round red
chillies on stems

Brussels sprouts and
Romanesco cauliflower
florets spiked on
bamboo sticks

Limequat

Squash

Scented white
hyacinth (below)
embedded in
a tank of damp
moss

"Paper white" narcissi
tied with raffia

Vase lined with sprigs
of spruce then filled
with florist's foam

KISSING BOUGH

THE CUSTOMARY EVERGREEN kissing bough is more than just a Christmas decoration: the juicy red apple in the centre symbolizes plenty and fertility for the coming season and, hung by the door, the bunch of mistletoe means no visitor can avoid a Christmas kiss! Pack the globe with evergreens, wire brightly coloured ribbons into bows and add gilded fruit, baubles and tiny Christmas tree decorations for extra festive punch.

Bunch of mistletoe with stems wired and tied with a ribbon

KISSING BOUGH Ingredients

5m (5½yd) steel wire

Carpet tape

Reel of fine wire

Apple

3cm (1¼in) bamboo stick

20cm (8in) gold thread

50cm (20in) thick cord

20 strands ivy

Making wired ribbon bows

Zig zag 15cm (6in) of ribbon into three small loops and pinch the ends. Twist a short piece of fine wire around the pinched ends, leaving enough spare to act as a stem. Make 10 of these bows for the kissing bough.

12 stems mistletoe

2m (2¼yd) tartan ribbon

50 artificial berries

♦ EQUIPMENT ♦

Wire-cutters

Pliers

Darning needle

Scissors

Red artificial berries
on wire stems

FORBIDDEN FRUIT
*Make the kissing bough
full to overflowing with
lush greenery, but ensure that
a tempting glimpse of the apple
can be caught between the boughs.*

MAKING THE KISSING BOUGH

The frame is easy to make using steel wire bought from a roll because it bends naturally into circles which can be held securely with strong carpet tape. Variegated ivy leaves lighten the overall colour; choose plain leaves if you require a more dense effect.

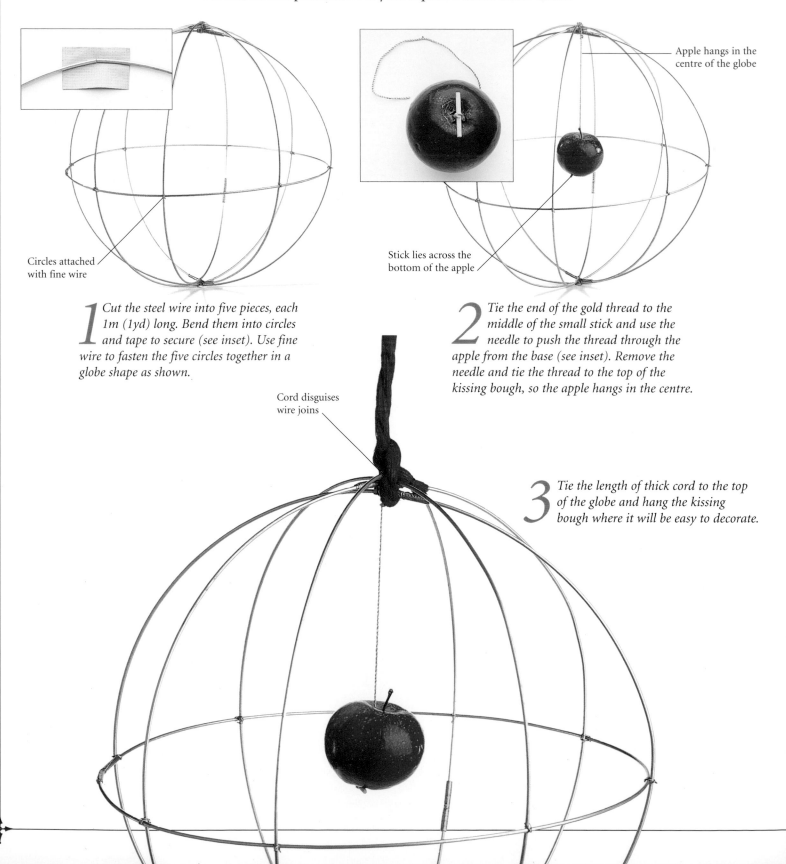

Circles attached with fine wire

Apple hangs in the centre of the globe

Stick lies across the bottom of the apple

Cord disguises wire joins

1 Cut the steel wire into five pieces, each 1m (1yd) long. Bend them into circles and tape to secure (see inset). Use fine wire to fasten the five circles together in a globe shape as shown.

2 Tie the end of the gold thread to the middle of the small stick and use the needle to push the thread through the apple from the base (see inset). Remove the needle and tie the thread to the top of the kissing bough, so the apple hangs in the centre.

3 Tie the length of thick cord to the top of the globe and hang the kissing bough where it will be easy to decorate.

Weave long strands
of ivy around the
wire circles

Mistletoe suspended
from bottom of globe

4 *Wind long strands of ivy around the
wire frame, using fine wire to secure
the pieces as necessary. Keep adding
ivy until the bough is as bushy as required,
but make sure the apple can still be seen.*

5 *Gather the mistletoe into a bunch,
secure the stems with wire and
overtie with 50cm (20in) ribbon.
Use a long tail of wire to hook the bunch
to the bottom of the ivy-covered globe.*

Apple can be
seen through
gaps in the ivy

Artificial berries
add colour

6 *Wire clusters of artificial berries to the
bough by their stems. Make 10 wired
ribbon bows (see page 68) and fix
them to the globe by their wire stems to
finish. Hang in position.*

FRUIT AND FLOWER DISPLAY

A MAGNIFICENT TOWER of spectacular fruit and flowers is guaranteed to turn a Christmas banquet into a feast for the eyes. Buy gilded walnuts on wires, twist stub wire through and around stems of roses and hypericum, and push it into lychees and berries in advance to secure them in the display.

MAKING THE DISPLAY

1 *Slice off the top 6cm (2½in) of the cone. Fasten the moss to the cone one handful at a time, wrapping the reel of wire around it to secure.*

FRUIT AND FLOWER DISPLAY Ingredients

♦ EQUIPMENT ♦

Kitchen knife

140 stub wires
(medium gauge)

25 large handfuls
loose moss

Cone of florist's foam,
20cm (8in)
base diameter,
50cm (20in) high

Reel of
fine wire

31 bamboo sticks, 25cm (10in)
long, broken into 92 lengths

8 plane leaves, sprayed gold

15 red apples

25 sharon fruit

27 plums

14 small pears

42 roses

30 lychees

14 gilded
walnuts

5 apricots

5 passion fruit

8 bunches
hypericum

70 ivy leaves

60 cranberries

1 mini pineapple

2 *Place the cone on a bed of gold plane leaves. Slipping short lengths of bamboo into the fruit as you work, push rings of skewered apples, sharon fruit and plums into the foam. Build up the display by adding rings of small pears, roses, lychees, more sharon fruit and plums.*

3 *Add more rings of gilded walnuts, apricots and passion fruit, lychees, roses and hypericum. To finish, add cranberries to fill gaps, slide ivy leaves between the layers and place the pineapple on a bamboo stick at the top.*

FESTIVE FRUIT
*Mix brightly coloured fruit in
different sizes and textures with
a few gilded nuts and leaves for
special Christmas glitter.*

Pineapple
skewered in place

Hypericum
decorates the top
few layers

Ring of ivy
leaves slipped
between the layers

Cranberries interspersed
among larger fruit

CHRISTMAS LIGHTS & EFFECTS

Lighting plays an important part in creating the right atmosphere for a party, be it old-fashioned candles smelling sweetly of beeswax, bright modern candles in a bold candelabra, or the romance of a chandelier made from twigs. Let quirky lanterns swing enticingly in the porch, beckoning guests inside where hand-made centrepieces and specially decorated mantelpieces provide a focus for the season's festivities.

AN ARRAY OF CANDLES

THE SOFT, FLICKERING LIGHT and evocative scent of a host of beautiful candles conjure up the ideal ambiance for a Christmas gathering. Choose from rolled beeswax, twisted, tapered or square candles, the traditional church variety, moulded novelties or floating flowery candles in festive colours. Reflect the opulence of the season by adorning complementary candle holders with twisted ribbons, cords and bows.

BEESWAX CANDLES

Choose exquisite beeswax candles for their natural texture and the delicious honey fragrance given off when they burn. Tie thin candles of differing heights together in small bundles to render candlesticks unnecessary.

FLOATING CANDLES

Make beautiful reflections with glittery flower-shaped candles floating in a wide-rimmed, shallow bowl. Scatter petals on the surface of the water for a truly luxurious feel.

Spiral candle decorated with a ring of sparkling glass droplets

Candles tied in bunches should not be lit

String of gold stars wrapped around candle holder

CANDLES IN HOLDERS
Support tall, graceful candles in holders made from glass and gilded wood, here decorated with chandelier-style droplets, twinkly gold stars and rich satin tassels.

FREE-STANDING CANDLES
Jazz up chunky, free-standing candles by adding ribbons and brocade, spiralling cord around them or tying a gold leaf to the front. Choose novelty candles with unusual shapes and finishes such as glossy or marbled gold.

Blue and gold
tassel adorns a
church candle

Ribbon and
gold-sprayed
oak leaves adorn
a chunky cream
candle

Sparkly gold elastic
wound around a
chunky candle

DECORATED CANDELABRAS

TRANSFORM A SIMPLE wrought-iron candelabra into a stunning table centrepiece by winding glossy evergreen leaves around the branched arms and scattering gold foil leaves among rich red roses. Adapt the idea with more dense foliage and artificial grapes, bright satin cord and coloured candles or, for a more formal party, dangle jewel-like beads below navy beeswax candles.

Satin cord hides the black candelabra

LUSH GREENERY
Enliven a candelabra with a bounteous display made by entwining glossy evergreen leaves among the branches. Hang bunches of lustred artificial grapes from the leaves and finish with pale green candles.

Christmas tree decoration

Tapered candle made of rolled beeswax

MEXICAN-STYLE CANDELABRA
Wind brightly coloured satin cord tightly around the branches of a black candelabra and add candles in colours to match. Glamorous Christmas tree decorations in matching colours give a festive feel.

EVENING ELEGANCE
Thread delicate blue glass beads and festive gold stars on to fine wire and wrap them in and out of the candelabra branches. Add movement with pretty drops hanging down, and finish with unusual midnight blue beeswax candles.

Hanging gold star catches the light

FRESH FLOWERS

A fresh arrangement made by winding ivy and roses around a candelabra creates a stunning centrepiece for a special party. If the display needs to last for the whole festive season, use artificial flowers and greenery instead.

Cream candles complement the dense colours

Gold foil leaves on wire stems from cake-decorating shops

Rich red rose wired to ivy and gold foil leaves

Wiring roses

Place an ivy leaf on its stem behind a rosebud so the two stems lie together. Push florist's wire through the bottom of the rosebud and wind it down around both stems to the bottom. Holding the wired stems in one hand and florist's tape in the other, twist the stems to wind the tape around them, binding them together.

TWIG CHANDELIER

GIVE A VINE WREATH a new lease of life by turning it into a
spectacular twig chandelier complete with burning candles.
Adorn it with dried fruit, chillies, gilded nuts and seed pods,
and add sparkling glass droplets to catch the light. Hang
your chandelier over the dinner table for elegant festive
dining or use the glass of a nearby mirror to reflect the
warm glow of the candles around the room.

TWIG CHANDELIER Ingredients

Twig wreath, sprayed gold

◆ EQUIPMENT ◆

Scissors

Strong glue

1.8m (2yd)
gold cord

9 candle
holders

Dried
mangosteen,
gilded

6 dried
tangerines,
gilded

1 pine
cone

15 large dried chillies

40 small
dried chillies

6 glass
droplets

6 wired bows

10 dried tropical
seed pods, gilded

4 pecans,
gilded

9 Christmas
tree candles

Dried tangerine with
gilding creme rubbed
on to the skin

BURNING BRIGHT
Never leave the twig chandelier burning unattended, and make sure you replace the candles as they burn down.

Tree decoration
or replacement
chandelier droplet
from a lighting shop

MAKING THE CHANDELIER

1 Cut the cord into three lengths of 60cm (24in). Tie them to the wreath equal distances apart and knot them together at the top. Clip the candle holders around the wreath.

2 Use a strong glue to attach the mangosteen, tangerines, pine cone, chillies, seed pods and pecans.

3 Hang the chandelier. Position the candles and glass droplets then add the wired bows to finish.

FROSTED CENTREPIECE

DELIGHT YOUR DINNER GUESTS with this abundant table centrepiece, smothered in sparkling sugar-frosted fruit that glitters in the candlelight. Use thick creamy candles, frosted fruit, candied peel, dried flowers and artificial berries in colours to complement the table setting. If all the fresh fruit is frosted, the centrepiece should last up to one week.

FROSTED CENTREPIECE Ingredients

◆ EQUIPMENT ◆

Knife

Scalpel

Metal ruler

40 stub wires
(medium gauge)

**Block florist's foam,
22.5 x 11 x 7.5cm
(9 x 4½ x 3¼in)**

**Silver cake board,
25 x 16cm (10 x 6½in)**

**2 candles,
16cm (6½in) high**

**1 candle,
24cm (9½in) high**

**15 sprigs
dried leaves**

**12 dried
hydrangea heads**

**10 bunches dried,
dyed broom**

17 poppy heads

**12 bunches
artificial berries**

**15 dried
pink rosebuds**

**20 dried
peach rosebuds**

**10 wired bows
(see page 68)**

**3 frosted
pears**

**4 slices candied
citron peel**

**7 small bunches
frosted grapes**

**Frosted
purple fig**

**Candied
green fig**

**2 candied
tangerines**

**Candied
greengage**

**6 frosted
kumquats**

**5 frosted slices
star fruit**

LIVING FLAME
Replace candles before they burn down to the level of the highest piece of fruit.

Candied fruit does not need frosting

Bow made with green ribbon (see page 68)

Rosebuds wired into bunches

MAKING THE FROSTED CENTREPIECE

Prepare the frosted fruit in advance to allow it time to dry (see
opposite), bend ribbon to make wired bows (see page 68) and
twist stub wire around the stems of small bunches of berries,
rosebuds and broom to secure them in the foam.

*1 Measure the diameter of the
candles, cut holes for them
in the cake board and place
it on the block of florist's foam.
Push the tallest candle through
the centre hole and flank with
the two shorter candles.*

*2 Push the sprigs of dried leaves and
hydrangea heads into the florist's
foam below the cake board.*

*3 Add the wired bunches of broom
and the poppy heads between the
dried leaves and hydrangeas.*

Push in items at different
angles to make the display
look more natural

1 Wash and dry the fruit to ensure that the skin is clean. Lightly whisk the whites of two eggs in a bowl and use a pastry brush to apply it to the prepared fruit skin.

4 *Fill in all the gaps by pushing the wire stems of the artificial berries and rosebuds into the florist's foam.*

Individual rosebuds wired into bunches

2 Use a spoon to sprinkle caster or finely granulated sugar gently over the fruit. This gives a more delicate, frosted look than rolling the fruit in sugar.

5 *Pile the frosted fruit and candied peel on the cake board to hide it from view completely. To finish, fill any gaps with a scattering of ribbon bows, fastened by pushing the wire stems into the foliage.*

3 Leave the fruit to dry on a wire rack. When frosted it will last for up to one week.

LANTERNS

A CLUSTER OF FESTIVE LANTERNS twinkling in
the porch guides guests to the front door at
Christmas. Buy lanterns ready-made and
embellish them with beads, fancy cords
and Christmas tree decorations, or make
your own using small glass jars and night-
light candles. Use glass paint in rich, jewel
colours, add shimmering stars and
snowflakes with gold paste, or try the
sponge-painting technique on page 126.

Right, from top to bottom:
MOONLIGHT LANTERN
*Spray a metal lantern with gold paint and
paint a red moon on one of the glass sides.*

RED AND GREEN POT
*Paint red and green stripes on a jam jar hung
from a simple wire harness threaded with beads.*

GREEN GARDEN LIGHT
*Wrap wire around the rim of a green glass
holder, and suspend it from a spiral of wire.*

Centre, from top to bottom:
TREE LANTERN
*Decorate a shop-bought lantern with red glass
paint and hang it from a length of green cord.*

FANCY LANTERN
*Embellish a shop-bought lantern with gold stars
painted on the glass and dangling beneath.*

LARGE RED LANTERN
*Hang a lustred moon from the bottom of a red-
painted tin lantern suspended from gold cord.*

Far right, from top to bottom:
GLOWING GREEN GLASS
*Place a small green glass in a shop-bought wire
holder decorated with luminous beads.*

STARLIGHT POT
*Paint coloured stars, moons and dots on a red
glass pot and hang it from a spiral of green wire.*

LARGE OUTDOOR LANTERN
*Paint gold stars on the glass of a dark green
lantern and add a tall cream candle.*

RED CANDLE-HOLDER
*Hook a loose spiral of wire around a tapered
glass holder and glue beads in place on the wire.*

ROCOCO MANTELPIECE

THE PLUSH VELVET on this sumptuous Christmas mantelpiece is punctuated with winter flowers in deep shades, jewel-coloured glasses and cut-glass tree decorations. Smother the shelf in a piece of rich velvet with gold braid sewn along the scalloped edge and add gilded accessories, opulent festive baubles and a garland made with wire-edged silk ribbons.

Beeswax candle suits matt gold wooden candlestick

Anemones, spray roses and scarlet nerines interspersed with loops of sparkly blue ribbon

Steel tin sprayed gold and filled with florist's foam

Fresh orange wrapped with braid secured with upholstery pins

Gilded picture frame
with braided edge
and blue velvet inset

Gold tree decoration
tied with gauzy ribbon

Decorative gold
wire shapes catch
the light

Red velvet pelmet
decorated with
silk ribbons

SILVER MANTELPIECE

THIS WINTRY LOOK is warmed by the glow of frosted glass oil lamps and decorated with festive silver accessories that gleam in the firelight. Adorn a pelmet of silver card with square paper doilies and variegated holly leaves, and add life with cream tulips and a tree of pale green leaves.

Painted wooden frame with inset of corrugated card and glass grapes

Elegant urn surrounded by a string of silver beads

Silver card pelmet trimmed with holly leaves, doilies and frosty baubles

Silver-green helichrysum
sprigs and silver baubles
pushed into florist's foam

Lid of a silver
star-shaped box

Silver and pearl
baubles in an
etched glass goblet

HOMESPUN MANTELPIECE

NATURAL COLOURS AND MATERIALS are central to this traditional look.
Dried citrus fruit, bunches of cinnamon sticks, pressed tin birds
and festive pastry-cutters sit on top of the mantel, and a garland
packed with dried fruit, nuts and salt dough
shapes (see page 20) hangs beneath.

Miniature Christmas
tree decorated with
tiny spice biscuits

Pastry-cutters
hung from
ribbon

Bay leaves
tacked to a
cotton ball

Painted wooden frame and checked fabric inset adorned with salt dough tree

Jolly star-shaped lollipops sit in a festive mug

Heart made of pressed tin

Plain church candles add simple style

Cones and wooden fruit fill a Christmas bowl

Tiny woven basket filled with foil-wrapped chocolate balls

SUNSHINE MANTELPIECE

A COLOURFUL DISPLAY brings the warmth of the sun to the Christmas festivities in your home. Choose real and paper flowers in the brightest colours and keep accessories natural in straw, pressed tin, wood and paper. Trim the mantel with easily made paper bunting to create a party mood, and echo the citrus shades with vibrant candles.

Coil of gold wire with stars

Heavy papier-mâché box containing ranunculus, poppies and gold-sprayed dried eucalyptus leaves

Paper rosettes glued
on to sticks, mixed
with gold moons
and bead flowers

Punched
tin vase

Blue wooden vase filled
with spice balls (see
page 30) and metal
fruit and vegetables

Tinplate
fish (see
page 46)

Seasonal Gifts, Cards & Stationery

A growing number of tell-tale white envelopes landing on the doormat heralds the approach of Christmas, when unique hand-crafted cards will be treasured by the recipient. Give gifts a special treatment too with stylish and witty hand-printed wrapping papers, and add complementary gift tags and clever decorations to prove that details really do count.

GIFT WRAP

MAKE GIFTS FOR FRIENDS and relatives extra special by designing your own sumptuous wrapping papers to shimmer enticingly under the tree. Print festive motifs on to coloured paper, or brush a thick paint and paste mixture over plain paper and scrape off interesting patterns. Buy rolls of inexpensive paper to work on, or be more extravagant with coloured tissue, textured and recycled paper.

BLOCK PRINTING Ingredients

Pencil eraser

Pastry cutter

Balsa wood

Cork

Paper

◆ EQUIPMENT ◆

Scalpel or craft knife

Glue

Paintbrush

Opaque waterproof paint

PASTE-GRAIN PAPER
Ingredients

Opaque waterproof paint

Thick card

Wallpaper paste

Paper

◆ EQUIPMENT ◆

Shallow bowl

Spoon or spatula

Wide paintbrush

Scissors

Cardboard block-print partridge with gold nail-head eye

Pencil eraser block print and nail-head berries

Pencil eraser block print

Coiled string and wooden block print

PRINTED PAPERS
*Transform plain or coloured paper into
eye-catching gift wrap with simple block
and paste-grain prints.*

Cardboard comb and
wooden block print

BLOCK PRINTING

Search the shops for wooden fabric-printing blocks to print with, or make your own from a pencil eraser. Natural sponges and coiled string can also be used to create interesting prints, or original designs can be cut from card or carved into potatoes.

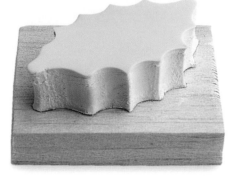

1 Push the pastry-cutter firmly through the pencil eraser to make a leaf-shaped rubber block for the stamp.

2 Cut a piece of balsa wood slightly larger than the rubber stamp and glue them together.

3 Carve extra detail, such as a vein, into the leaf. Trim the cork and glue it to the balsa wood to act as a handle.

Add details such as holly berries using knitting needles or nail heads dipped in paint

4 Brush some paint on to the stamp, avoiding the carved detail, and press on to the paper to print.

PRETTY PRINTS
Liven up plain red sugar paper with colourful clusters of leaves. Add gold berries for festive extravagance.

Other Ideas

Cardboard stamp
Draw a motif on a piece of card and cut it out. Glue it to a larger piece of card and attach a cork to the back as a handle.

String print
Coil a piece of string, press it on to some glued paper and cut around it. Secure a cork to the back.

Potato print
Cut a potato in half and use a small kitchen knife to cut a pattern into the cut side of one half.

Sponge print
Dip a natural sponge lightly into gold paint and dab on paper for a shimmery effect.

MAKING PASTE-GRAIN PAPER

A thick mixture of wallpaper paste and paint gives rich colour and texture to plain paper. Scrape away eye-catching patterns with a comb cut from cardboard at least 2mm (¹⁄₁₆in) thick or use different household objects for a range of effects.

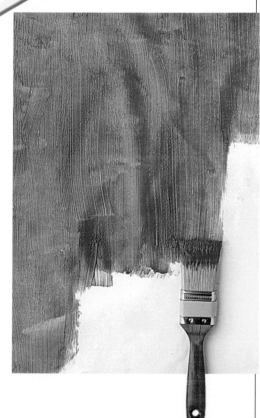

1 In a shallow bowl, mix some wallpaper paste with water according to the instructions on the packet.

2 Once the paste has thickened, gradually mix paint into it until it reaches the desired colour.

3 Use a wide paintbrush to coat the paper with the mixture. Brush it on roughly for a textured effect.

4 Cut thick card into a comb shape and use it to scrape a swirling or zig zag pattern into the wet paint and paste mixture. Leave to dry.

Swirling pattern made with 6-tooth comb

Other Ideas

Printing block
Press a clean wooden fabric-printing block on to the wet paint and paste. Add squiggly lines using a pastry wheel.

Pastry wheel
Run a pastry wheel across wet paint and paste for wiggly lines.

Fork
Choose a fork with equal length prongs for a simple yet stunning effect. Wash the fork carefully after use.

GIFT BOXES

ADD A HINT OF MYSTERY to a special gift by presenting it in a luxurious made-to-measure box. Choose card in colours that complement the gift and hand-print it with festive designs (see pages 100-101) for an even more personal touch. Gauzy ribbons tied in lush bows, or rich gold cord and tassels, offer a final flourish for a truly elegant box.

MAKING A RECTANGULAR BOX

Vary the measurements given on the template above to suit the size of your gift.

RECTANGULAR BOX Ingredients

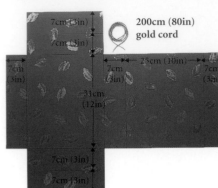

7cm (3in)
7cm (3in)
200cm (80in) gold cord
7cm (3in)
7cm (3in)
25cm (10in)
7cm (3in)
31cm (12in)
7cm (3in)
7cm (3in)
25cm (10in)

TEMPLATE
Patterned or coloured card, 59 x 71cm (24 x 29in)

The measurements given here make the largest of the rectangular boxes shown.

◆ EQUIPMENT ◆

Pencil

Plastic ruler

Cutting mat

Scalpel or craft knife

Metal ruler

Glue (optional)

Single-hole punch

1 Using a pencil and ruler, mark out the dimensions given on the template on to the decorated side of the card.

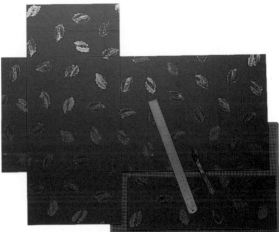

2 Place the card on a cutting mat and use a scalpel or sharp craft knife and metal ruler to cut carefully around the outside edge of the template as shown.

3 Align the metal ruler with the remaining pencil lines and score lightly along each one.

4 Fold the card inward along the scored lines to create a box. To close it, tie gold cord or ribbon around the box. It is not necessary to glue the box closed, but it will be more secure if you do.

Pyramid Box Ingredients

45cm (18in) ribbon

TEMPLATE
Patterned or coloured card, 54 x 54cm (21 x 21in)

18cm (7in)

18cm (7in)

18cm (7in)

The measurements given here make the small pyramid in the foreground.

PYRAMID BOX

Mark out the template on card, then cut and score as for the rectangular box. Using a single-hole punch, make a hole in each of the four points. Thread a ribbon through the holes, gently pull the points together and tie in a simple bow.

FESTIVE BOXES

Wrap gifts in layers of coloured tissue paper and tie the boxes loosely to show a splash of colour within.

Square box

Small rectangular box

Tall pyramid

Large rectangular box

Small pyramid

RIBBONS & BOWS

FINISH A BEAUTIFULLY WRAPPED parcel with a length of lavish ribbon tied in a generous bow. Experiment with interesting brocade, raffia and strings of glitzy sequins, or visit stationery shops for paper ribbons in unusual colours and textures. Be creative with romantic flower bows and opulent double bows, or make it quick and easy with a simple cheat's bow.

Twisted paper

Coarse-weave wire-edged ribbon

Shot taffeta with gold wire edge

Wire-edged organza

WIRE-EDGED RIBBONS
Use a wire-edged ribbon to make a pretty rose-shaped bow, as well as to give support to all other types of bow.

Wire-edged striped taffeta

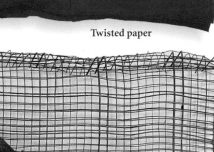

Open weave jute

Curling ribbon

Plaited flat cord

Gold-flecked tissue paper

PAPER RIBBONS
Look in stationery shops for paper ribbons in a variety of textures guaranteed to add interest to gift wrapping.

Cotton webbing

Single-faced velvet

Flat green taffeta

Double-faced satin

FLAT RIBBONS
Satin or velvet ribbons are ideal for making elegant flat bows.

Woven gold cord

Gimp edging

Single row sequins

CORDS AND SEQUINS
Try the haberdashery department of a large store for more unusual types of ribbon.

Organza with gold edging

ORGANZA RIBBONS
Wispy organza ribbons make exquisite bows for glamorous gifts.

Organza with taffeta stripes

CHEAT'S BOW Using wire-edged ribbon

1 Make a loop in the centre of the ribbon and hold it where the tails cross.

2 Pull the top of the loop down behind the cross to form two small loops.

3 Wrap a long piece of wire around the middle of the bow to secure it.

Trim the ends of the ribbon as required

DOUBLE BOW Using wire-edged ribbon

1 Holding the ribbon at its centre, bring half of the left tail up underneath to make a loop. Hold it in position. Repeat to make a second, slightly larger loop underneath.

2 Hold the loops in place with your left hand and repeat step 1 using the right-hand tail of ribbon to make two loops. Pinch all four loops in the centre to hold.

3 Fold a short piece of the same ribbon in half lengthways and wrap around the centre of the bow. Twist a wire around the two ends at the back to secure.

Trim the ends of the ribbon diagonally

ROSE BOW Using wire-edged ribbon and beaded wire stamens

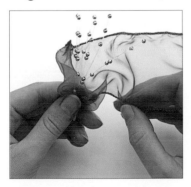  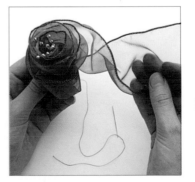 

1 Hold the bottom of the wire stamens in one hand and start to wind the ribbon loosely around them in a circle, pinching the bottom.

2 After each wrap, sew a few small stitches in the bottom to hold the bow together. Continue wrapping, fanning out the top as you go.

3 Near the end of the ribbon, twist it as you wrap to create a petal effect. Tuck the end down toward the bottom and sew to secure.

Fluff out the top of the rose to make it look flower-like

FINISHING TOUCHES

SMALL CHRISTMAS TREE DECORATIONS, artificial berries, dried fruit and flowers, shells, pieces of costume jewellery and little trinkets are all worth saving to make into original accessories for wrapped gifts. Glue or wire unusual knick-knacks together to complement or boldly contrast with the style of the wrapping, then tape or hook the arrangement to a decorative ribbon and remember to add a quirky home-made gift tag (see page 110).

NATURAL ITEMS

Pine cone

Holly leaf

Dried orange segment

Polished shells

Cinnamon sticks

Dried rosebud

ARTIFICIAL ITEMS

Artificial berries

Gold brocade tree decoration

Artificial pearls

Strips of silver corrugated card

Blue beads threaded on wire

Cluster of artificial berries

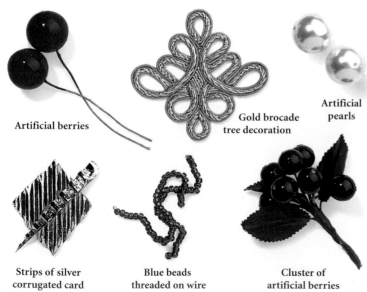

Gold brocade decoration acts as a mount for the tassel

GOLD AND GLITZY
Create this opulent festive accessory by gluing together two shop-bought Christmas tree decorations.

Luxurious gold tassel shimmers in the light

Slices of orange dried on a flat surface

FRUIT CLUSTER
Three slices of dried orange glued together look attractive topped with cheat's bows made from copper-coloured satin and organza ribbon (see page 105).

White paper flowers
sprayed gold

Gold stamens
from a cake
decorating shop

Dark green
mesh ribbon
enhances the
outdoor theme

GILDED POSY
*Twist the stems of gold paper flowers and
stamens together with loops of gold ribbon. Add
a touch of colour with blue beads threaded on wire,
and bind all the stems with gold cord to secure.*

Silver cord
loops

SEASHELLS AND PEARLS
*Glue shells, pearls and a bunch of
lustred artificial grapes to an oval of silver
corrugated card, and top with flat silver cord
gathered into loops.*

TRADITIONAL HOLLY
*Tie cinnamon sticks together with a bow
made from open-weave ribbon, then attach
with wire to stems of holly. Dried rosebuds
secured with gold thread and wired to the
front of the bow add a decorative detail.*

Shop-bought
artificial berries

Bound stems of
paper rose and
artificial berries

FESTIVE BERRIES
*Bind the stems of bunches
of artificial berries to a red
paper rose and glue a red
cheat's bow (see page 105)
and a pine cone to the front.*

BRONZE BOW
*Loop a wire-edged organza ribbon to make
a rosette and secure with wire at the back.
A cedar cone glued to the centre provides a
contrast in texture.*

LUXURY WRAPPINGS

STEAL THE LIMELIGHT under the Christmas tree with imaginatively wrapped gifts that make use of the wide range of unusual papers available in craft shops. Mix and match colours, textures and fabrics, and add panache with silk and satin ribbons, exotic feathers, glittery stars and shiny baubles. For a stylish, natural look try brown paper, dried seed pods and pressed leaves, or contrast a glitzy wrapping and a single leaf for maximum impact.

OTHER IDEAS

THE NATURAL LOOK
Glue a random pattern of dried leaves to textured brown paper. Tie with plaited raffia, adding loose strands tied in a bow on top. Finish the look with a dried mangosteen.

A TOUCH OF GLAMOUR
Tie red foil crêpe paper with a wide orange taffeta ribbon and top it with a red rose bow made from silk ribbon (see page 105). A dried leaf contrasts with the elegant swirls of the chiffon ribbon tucked beneath the bow.

SHIMMERING STARS
Cover dark purple crêpe paper with glassine paper to give a glossy effect. Tie a lush satin ribbon in a bow and add silver rick-rack braid. Mount a glittery star on wire and attach it to the ribbon to twinkle enticingly.

MAGIC AND MYSTERY
Gather a large rectangle of stiff fabric such as dupion silk around the gift and tie with a contrasting silk ribbon. Hint at festive decadence with two exotic feathers tucked under the ribbon.

WHITE BOX Ingredients

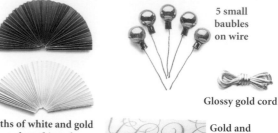

5 small baubles on wire

Glossy gold cord

Lengths of white and gold paper pleated into fans

Gold and white wrapping paper

Strips of pleated white paper

Strips of pleated paper opened into ribbons and tucked or glued under the fans and baubles

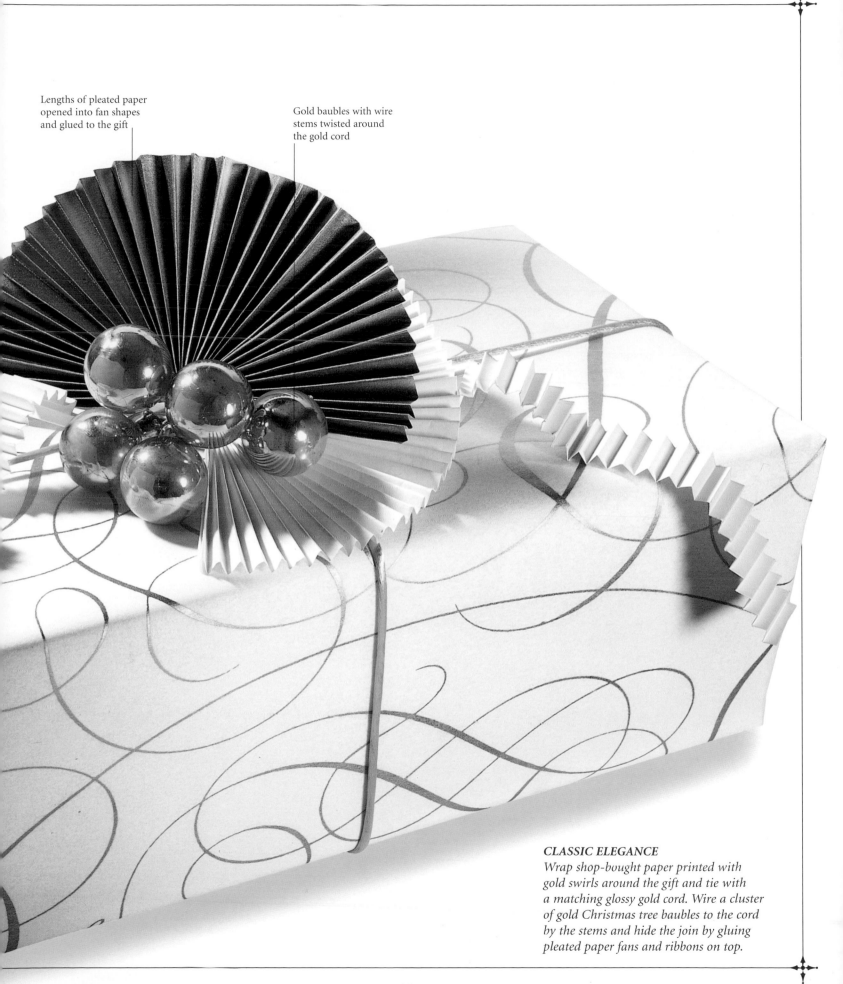

Lengths of pleated paper opened into fan shapes and glued to the gift

Gold baubles with wire stems twisted around the gold cord

CLASSIC ELEGANCE
Wrap shop-bought paper printed with gold swirls around the gift and tie with a matching glossy gold cord. Wire a cluster of gold Christmas tree baubles to the cord by the stems and hide the join by gluing pleated paper fans and ribbons on top.

GIFT TAGS

STYLISH GIFT TAGS add the final touch to beautifully wrapped Christmas presents. Try mixing natural textured papers, dried leaves and seed pods with wire shapes, sealing wax and festive decorations; emboss shapes on plain paper; or make block prints to match gift wrap. Tiny details make all the difference so cut quirky holes and tie with unusual scraps of ribbon, braid or string.

DECORATIVE DETAILS

FANCY SHAPES
Draw a shape in pencil and cut it out carefully using a scalpel or craft knife.

HOLE REINFORCEMENT
Glue a small circle of card to the gift tag and punch a hole through both layers. Use brown string as a tie.

RIBBON AND SEAL
Loop a piece of cord and dip it into warmed sealing wax. Place it on the paper and press a nail head into the wax to secure.

Dried poppy seed head

Holly leaf block print

Gold braid and sealing wax

Wire heart and reinforced hole

Embossed bird on corrugated card

Recycled paper leaf outlined in gold pen

Gold star on marbled paper with square hole

Potato print heart

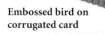

Gold foil leaf

Embossed heart with heart-shaped hole

Embossed leaf with a triangular hole

Dried hydrangea head

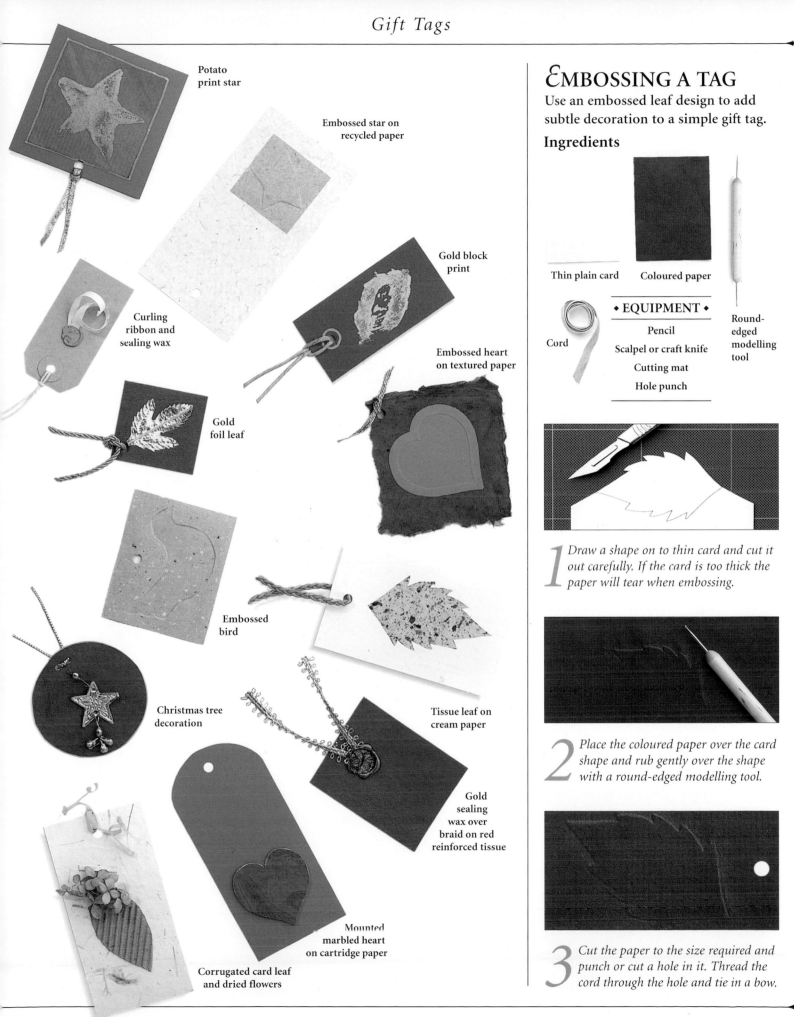

Potato print star

Embossed star on recycled paper

Gold block print

Curling ribbon and sealing wax

Embossed heart on textured paper

Gold foil leaf

Embossed bird

Christmas tree decoration

Tissue leaf on cream paper

Gold sealing wax over braid on red reinforced tissue

Mounted marbled heart on cartridge paper

Corrugated card leaf and dried flowers

EMBOSSING A TAG

Use an embossed leaf design to add subtle decoration to a simple gift tag.

Ingredients

Thin plain card   Coloured paper

Cord

Round-edged modelling tool

◆ EQUIPMENT ◆

Pencil

Scalpel or craft knife

Cutting mat

Hole punch

1 Draw a shape on to thin card and cut it out carefully. If the card is too thick the paper will tear when embossing.

2 Place the coloured paper over the card shape and rub gently over the shape with a round-edged modelling tool.

3 Cut the paper to the size required and punch or cut a hole in it. Thread the cord through the hole and tie in a bow.

CHRISTMAS CARDS

THE BEAUTY OF THESE EYE-CATCHING Christmas cards lies in their simplicity. Start collecting interesting papers and cards, pretty pieces of ribbon and braid, tiny beads from unwanted necklaces and shiny gold decorations and use them to create unique cards for friends and family.

COLLAGE CARD
Decorate festive red sugar paper with torn squares of rough textured paper. Create depth by gathering a small piece of gold wire-edged ribbon into a flower shape and gluing it on top.

Gummed foil cupids from stationery shops

SWIRLS AND CUPIDS
Cut a piece of hand-decorated paper (see page 101) and glue it to textured card in a contrasting colour. Finish with gold foil cupids in a random pattern.

KNOT AND BRAID CARD
Glue a snippet of heavy metallic braid and a knot of metallic gold cord to textured red card. A small piece of metal ribbon glued across the top of the braid prevents fraying.

BIJOU BOWS
Loop gold brocade into a bow and attach to turquoise card. For added interest tuck a gold leaf beneath the bow (see centre card).

Gold beads secured
with glue

RECYCLED LOOK
*Juxtapose torn recycled paper with
luxurious cream card and cover with
a scattering of small gold beads.*

CARD AND CORD
*Glue recycled cream paper to finely
corrugated brown card and add
a loop of gold cord. Sketch a design
in pencil and accentuate it with
small gold beads glued over the top.*

Beads glued in
place over a
design sketched
in pencil

TEXTURED PAPER
*Beautifully textured hand-made
paper hardly needs extra
embellishment. Simply add a
brown corrugated card leaf to
continue the natural theme.*

PAPYRUS EFFECT
*Glue layers of papyrus to cream
ribbed card. Cut two tiny slots
in the centre, pass the wires of a
gold foil leaf through both slots
and tape at the back to secure.*

PATTERNED LEAF
*Cut a leaf shape from
hand-decorated paper (see page
101) and attach it diagonally
across a piece of sugar paper in
contrasting brick red.*

NOVELTY CARDS

DELIGHTFUL NOVELTY CARDS like this bejewelled festive tree and woolly sheep with its beady eye are deceptively easy to make using the templates on pages 187–88. Let your imagination run riot with alternative designs, and experiment with exciting materials to create highly original cards that will delight the children and take pride of place on the mantelpiece at Christmas.

NOVELTY CARDS Ingredients

Thin green wire

Cream curling ribbon

Brown curling ribbon

Green card, plain card and textured paper

Small beads

◆ EQUIPMENT ◆

Pencil

Scalpel or craft knife

Cutting mat

Metal ruler

Scissors

Glue

MAKING THE TREE Using the template on page 187

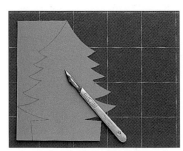

1 Copy the template on to green card and cut it out carefully using a scalpel.

2 Turn the card over and score vertically down the centre with a scalpel. Fold it in half.

3 Cut three wires, each long enough to join both sides of the card. Thread tiny beads on to the wires, twisting a small loop after every few.

4 Make three tiny holes in each side of the tree (see inset). Push the ends of the wires through to the back and twist a loop at each end to secure.

MAKING THE SHEEP Using the template on page 188

1 Copy the template on to plain card and cut it out. Score a line across the centre fold.

2 Cut out the sheep's coat from textured paper and glue it on. Fold the sheep inward along the score-line so it can stand.

3 Curl short lengths of ribbon and glue them to the sheep's body. To finish, glue on a loosely curled ribbon as a horn and a bead for the eye.

AUTHENTIC TOUCHES
Delight children with a sheep that really rocks and a Christmas tree with jewel-like beads strung between the branches.

Twists in the wire separate the beads and allow movement

Fleecy coat made from curled ribbon

Curved base acts as a rocker

MENUS & INVITATIONS

CREATE PERSONAL INVITATIONS and menu cards using thin card embellished with rich satin cords or silvery ribbons woven in and out of slits and tied in jaunty bows. Enliven simple designs with quirky details such as unusually textured card, tiny square holes or fancy silver stitching and use the same techniques, scaled down, to make place names for a dinner party.

MENU CARD Ingredients

Card for inset

Card for frame

Ribbon

◆ EQUIPMENT ◆

Ruler

Scissors

Pencil

Scalpel or craft knife

Metal ruler

Cutting mat

Masking tape

Sewing on card

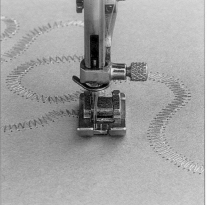

Cut the card to the size required before you begin, then thread the sewing machine with metallic silver thread and select zig zag stitch. As you sew, carefully move the card around, like a piece of fabric, to produce decorative swirls of silver stitching.

Silver voile ribbon threaded through two slits in a corrugated frame

Shop-bought frame decorated with ribbon threaded through slits

Ribbon threaded through two slits in the frame and tied in a bow

Machine zig zag stitch in silver thread

MAKING THE MENU CARD

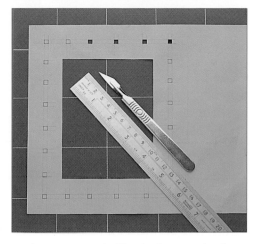

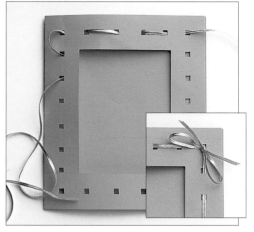

1 Cut out a suitable-sized rectangle of card and fold in half. Open it out and draw the frame in pencil on the front. Measure tiny squares around it and cut them out carefully using a scalpel and metal ruler.

2 Starting at the top right hand corner, thread the ribbon in and out of the square slots around the edge of the frame. When you reach the top again, tie both ends of the ribbon in a bow (see inset).

3 Write the menu on different coloured card and cut it out. Tape it in position behind the frame using two small pieces of masking tape so it can be removed and replaced if re-using the frame.

SHORT CUTS
If time is of the essence, buy card frames from stationery shops, glue on gift wrap to decorate and use a hole punch instead of a scalpel to make tiny holes for ribbons.

Silver braid threaded through slots cut with a scalpel

Wrapping paper glued to thin card with velvet ribbon threaded down one side

Checked voile ribbon in a shop-bought frame

Silver zig zag stitch frame

Satin cord wound around the edges of the frame

Hand-made paper with a rough texture

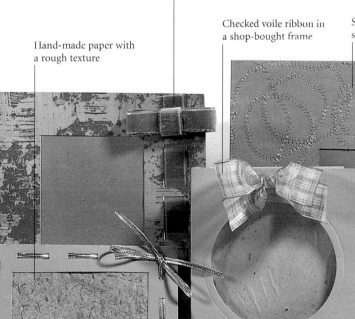

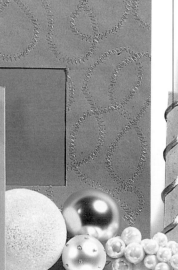

STOCKINGS

A GLIMPSE OF A TEMPTING PRESENT peeking from the top of a brightly coloured home-made Christmas stocking is enough to make any child's heart race with anticipation on Christmas morning. Sew or glue buttons, ribbons, felt shapes and strings of beads to the cuffs for festive decoration and trim the edges with pinking shears for added interest.

STAR STOCKING Ingredients

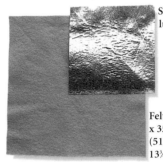

Silver lurex

Matching thread

Felt, 130 x 35cm (51 x 13¾in)

Beads

◆ EQUIPMENT ◆

Rough paper

Pencil

Scissors

Pins

Sewing machine or needle and thread

Pinking shears

Iron-on backing

Fabric glue

MAKING THE STAR STOCKING

TEMPLATE

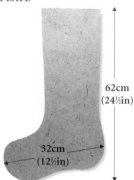

62cm (24½in)

32cm (12½in)

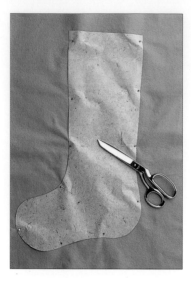

1 Copy the template on to rough paper and cut it out. Fold the felt in half and pin the template to it. Cut around the template through the double layer of felt.

SHINY STARS
Glue silver lurex stars to sea-green felt and add pearl beads to the centre of each star.

MINI BOWS
Sew bows of flat silver ribbon to the stocking top and glue tiny pearls to the centre of each.

RIBBONS AND ROPES
Use tiny stitches to secure wide checked ribbon, paper rope and a narrow silver ribbon around the cuff of the stocking.

LOVE HEART
Cut a simple heart from bright pink felt and use fabric glue to secure it to a contrasting green miniature stocking.

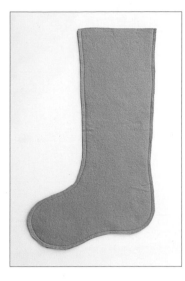

2 Sew the two felt stockings together around the edges, leaving the top open.

3 Cut around all the edges, including the top, with pinking shears.

4 Turn the top of the stocking inside out to make a cuff. Cut stars from silver lurex and glue them to the cuff. If the lurex frays, iron on a backing first.

5 Cut a small strip from the left-over felt and fold it in half. Sew it to the inside of the stocking cuff to make a secure loop for hanging.

SNOWY DROPS
Sew a string of tiny pearl beads along the top edge of the stocking, and glue or sew larger pearl beads and crystal drops randomly on the cuff.

BUTTONS
Fix a selection of pearl and glass buttons to the felt. Pack them more closely for a richer look.

CLASSIC PEARLS
Cut a necklace of tiny pearly beads to size and stitch it around the cuff of a sized-down stocking.

FESTIVE FELT TREES
Attach felt trees and pots to the stocking with glue. Decorate with tiny beads.

SILVER RIBBON
Glue two bands of flat silver ribbon around the top of the stocking for quick and easy style.

GIFT-FILLED ADVENT CALENDAR

THIS ENCHANTING FABRIC advent calendar consists of 24 small pockets, each decorated with a checked appliqué shape or number (see templates on pages 186–87). Stuff the pockets with little wooden toys, foil-wrapped sweets, gingerbread shapes, miniature crackers and gold-painted nuts that are sure to delight a child in the exciting days before Christmas.

Ingredients

Scraps of fabric

Felt, 106 x 45cm (42½ x 18in)
Backing material,
150 x 45cm
(60 x 18in)

Beads

2 x 10cm (4in) strips fringing

Ribbon

57cm (22in) wooden cane

82cm (32½in) cord

24 gifts

◆ EQUIPMENT ◆

Ruler
Scissors
Iron
Pen
Sewing machine
Needle and thread
Fabric glue
Pins

MAKING THE ADVENT CALENDAR

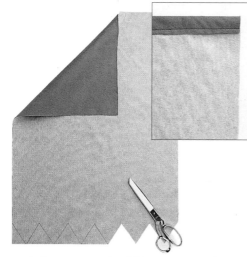

1 *Cut a rectangle of felt, 70 x 45cm (27½ x 18in). Iron on the backing material. Mark and cut a zig zag pattern across the bottom. Fold the top 3cm (1¼in) over and sew it in place to make a tube (see inset).*

2 *Cut four strips of felt, each 9 x 45cm (3¾ x 18in). Pin them across the rectangle, equal distances apart, then sew along the bottom and up the sides of each strip, leaving the tops open.*

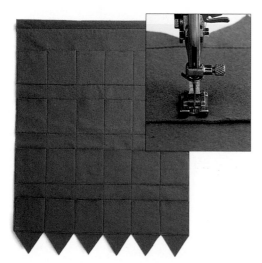

3 *Divide the horizontal strips into six equally sized pouches for the gifts by sewing a vertical line from the bottom of the bottom strip to the top of the top strip every 7.5cm (3in) across.*

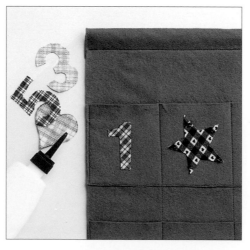

4 *Iron backing material on to the appliqué fabric and cut out numbers between 1 and 24 and small festive shapes. Decorate the pockets by gluing on a shape or number, and ribbons, bows or beads.*

5 *Roll the fringing into two tassels and sew to the ends of the cord. Thread the cane through the top of the calendar and tie the cord to each end. Finish, if desired, by sewing padded shapes along the bottom.*

FESTIVE FABRICS
Choose muted sea-green felt and simple ginghams for an understated country feel.

Tiny bows made from ribbon

Embellish the bottom of the calendar, if wished, with fabric shapes stuffed with cotton wool

The Dining Table

Boisterous parties, extravagant
feasts or quiet suppers with friends and
family focus the season's celebrations in
a very special way. Usually there is at least
one important meal that demands a beautifully
presented table. Either work around the table
settings you own, or choose a festive theme
as a starting point, then create a feast for the
eyes with an exquisite candle centrepiece,
decorated crockery, patterned table linen and
stunning home-made accessories.

BAROQUE TABLE SETTING

RICH, OPULENT AND WARM, in tones of claret and gold, this table setting is ideal for a sophisticated Christmas meal. A thick brocade cloth, shot silk napkins and antique bone-handled cutlery are complemented by simple glass dishes and goblets decorated with gold paint. A festive arrangement of lilies and evergreen leaves presides over the table and clusters of winter berries in gold-painted terracotta pots add the finishing touch.

DECORATED GLASS BOWL Ingredients

Sponge

Glass bowl

◆ EQUIPMENT ◆

White spirit

Soft cloth

Paintbrush

Scissors

Dish for paint

Red glass paint

Gold glass paint

GOLD FILIGREE GOBLET Ingredients

Gold contour-lining paste

Goblet

Sponge

Gold glass paint

◆ EQUIPMENT ◆

White spirit

Soft cloth

Dish for paint

Scissors

ADDITIONAL LUXURIES

Fill brass bowls with chocolates and almonds wrapped in gold foil, and place thick cream candles in wooden candle holders painted matt gold. Tie napkins with strings of gold beads.

DECORATING THE GLASS BOWL

Glass paints in rich jewel colours such as red and gold are ideal for decorating glassware at Christmas. If you intend to use the decorated items, choose durable non-toxic paints and avoid painting areas that will come into contact with food.

A fine-tipped paintbrush gives precision when applying paint to tiny areas

1 Prepare the glass surface for painting by cleaning it carefully with white spirit on a soft cloth.

2 Use a fine paintbrush to apply red glass paint to the underside of the pattern on the rim of the bowl. Take care not to smudge the paint on to the bowl itself, but if you do, wipe it off quickly.

Use a large sponge cut down: the tiny holes in a small sponge give too dense a pattern

Dab the paint gently on to the glass

3 Pour a small amount of gold paint into a shallow dish or saucer. Cut a small piece of sponge.

4 Dip the sponge into a little paint and press it randomly on to the underside of the bowl. Leave to dry.

DECORATING THE GOBLET

The swirly gold pattern on this goblet is reminiscent of
traditional gold filigree work. Achieve the effect by applying
contour-lining paste straight from the tube to the outside
of the goblet and the rim of a plate.

1 Prepare the glass surface for painting by cleaning it carefully with white spirit on a soft cloth.

2 Draw random swirly lines on the side of the goblet with contour-lining paste. Squeeze it carefully to prevent blobs.

3 Draw lines on the base of the glass to create a filigree-style pattern, taking care not to make smudges.

4 Use a sponge to decorate the stem of the glass with gold paint, following the instructions for step 4 opposite.

Decorated Plate

Remove any grease marks from a plate with a
little white spirit on a soft cloth. Use a tube of
contour-lining paste to decorate the rim of the
plate in a style to match the goblet.

NATURAL TABLE SETTING

THE NATURAL MATERIALS AND EARTHY TONES of this fresh and stylish look lend themselves to a festive lunch. Dress the table up with gleaming brass and white china plates, lustred gold glasses and wooden-handled cutlery, and echo the use of shop-bought preserved and gold-sprayed oak leaves by adding a gold leaf motif to the linen tablecloth and napkins.

PRINTED TABLECLOTH Ingredients

Leaf

Paper

Tablecloth

◆ EQUIPMENT ◆

Pencil

Scissors

Kitchen knife

Paintbrush

Towel

Potato

Gold fabric paint

GOLD LEAF NAPKINS Ingredients

Leaf

Paper

Gold cord

◆ EQUIPMENT ◆

Pencil

Scissors

Pen

Needle and gold thread

Embroidery scissors

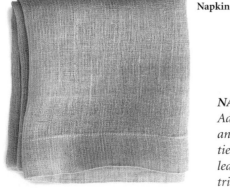
Napkin

NATURAL BEAUTY

Adorn the table with a simple wreath of leaves and twigs, an ornamental cabbage, and napkins tied with brown string, gold thread and oak leaves. Present each guest with a small gold trinket box decorated with a golden oak leaf.

PRINTING THE TABLECLOTH

Cutting the potato into a square shape and using a tablecloth with a regular pattern such as checks or stripes will help you position the prints straight. Alternatively, choose a plain cloth and add an abstract pattern of prints.

Align the straight edges of the potato with the checks on the tablecloth to keep the print straight

1 Choose a suitable leaf, either fresh or preserved, to use as a guide. Place it on the paper, draw around it and cut out.

2 Cut the potato in half and place the paper leaf on the flat edge. Cut around it with a kitchen knife.

3 Cut the potato into a rectangular shape around the leaf. Cut a detail such as a vein into the surface of the leaf.

4 Brush gold paint on to the cut leaf pattern, avoiding the carved-out detail.

5 Place an old towel or piece of fabric under the tablecloth, align the edges of the potato with the checks, and press it on to the cloth to print.

DECORATING THE NAPKIN

An oak leaf motif outlined in gold cord on each napkin
complements the prints on the tablecloth. Attach the motif
with tiny gold stitches and decorate the napkins with oak
leaves tied with brown string and gold thread.

1 Choose a leaf to use as a guide.
Draw and cut out a paper leaf
template as step 1 opposite.

2 Draw around the paper
template on to the napkin.
Lay the gold cord around
the leaf outline to measure how
much will be needed and cut it.

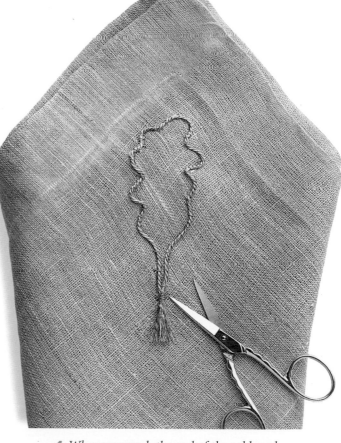

Use embroidery
scissors to fray
tassels at the ends
of the gold cord

Anchor the cord
with tiny stitches
in gold thread

3 Tie a knot near each end of the gold cord
and fray the ends into tassels. Sew the cord
around the leaf using gold thread.

4 When you reach the end of the gold cord,
sew across both ends a few times to secure.
Trim the tassels.

FIESTA TABLE SETTING

THE VIBRANT COLOURS of this table setting are perfect for a jubilant Christmas party. An array of plates and dishes in the brightest colours adorn a woven silk tablecloth with multi-coloured stripes, and shimmering shot organza napkins, frosted glassware and translucent yellow-handled cutlery contrast with the dense colours of the scalloped chinaware and papier-mâché plates and bowls.

PAPER PLATE Ingredients

5 sheets coloured tissue paper

Small paper plate

Wallpaper paste

Non-toxic, water-based varnish

◆ EQUIPMENT ◆

Mixing bowl
Spoon for mixing
Wide paintbrush
Medium paintbrush

PAPIER-MACHE BOWL Ingredients

China bowl

White paper

10 sheets coloured tissue paper

◆ EQUIPMENT ◆

Mixing bowl
Clingfilm
Spoon for mixing
Scissors
Wide paintbrush
Medium paintbrush

Wallpaper paste

Non-toxic, water-based varnish

EDIBLE CENTREPIECES
Arrange brightly coloured chillies, squashes, kumquats and limes in jazzy bowls and dishes.

COVERING THE PAPER PLATE

Cover inexpensive paper plates with brightly coloured tissue to ensure tableware is a perfect match for other festive accessories. When coated with non-toxic varnish, the plates will be suitable for dry foods, making them ideal for buffets.

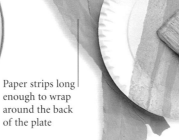

Paper strips long enough to wrap around the back of the plate

1 Mix the wallpaper paste according to the instructions on the packet. Tear the tissue paper into 2.5cm (1in) strips.

2 Use a wide brush to paste strips in one direction across the plate, so they overlap each other slightly.

3 When the plate is covered, paste another layer of strips across the plate in the opposite direction.

Water-based varnish gives a hard finish

4 Let the plate dry slowly, cover the back in strips if you wish, then varnish.

Napkin Rings

Wind strips of tissue coated with wallpaper paste around a napkin ring to cover it inside and out. Let it dry slowly so it does not buckle, then varnish as for the plate.

MAKING THE PAPIER-MACHE BOWL

Use papier-mâché to make bright bowls that are perfect for
serving finger foods. Hold the first layer of white paper in
position with water, not paste, to prevent it from
sticking to the clingfilm on the china bowl.

Overlap white paper strips
in all directions to give the
bowl extra strength

1 Wrap the china bowl in clingfilm.
Mix the wallpaper paste according to
the instructions on the packet. Tear the
white paper and tissue paper into long strips
2.5cm (1in) wide.

2 Turn the bowl upside down. Dip strips
of white paper in water, not wallpaper
paste, and place them, slightly
overlapping each other, in one direction
across the underside of the bowl.

3 When the bowl
is covered with one layer of paper, coat
more strips in wallpaper paste and place
them the opposite way across the bowl, using
a wide brush to flatten them. Leave to dry.

4 When the paper is completely dry,
remove the china bowl and trim the
top edge of the paper with scissors.

5 Cover the paper bowl inside and out
with strips of tissue paper coated in
paste, as steps 2 and 3 opposite.

6 Let the paper bowl dry, then varnish
the inside. When dry, turn it over and
varnish the outside.

MODERN TABLE SETTING

A CRISP, MODERN LOOK USING STARS, silver and delicate pastels is ideal for New Year's Eve. A pale lemon brushed cotton tablecloth provides a neutral background for lustrous checked silk napkins, star-shaped napkin rings, pale crockery, silver-sided glasses and gleaming cutlery. Hot-pink gerberas with silver star collars that match the astral coasters bring unexpected warmth to the cool feel of the table.

CANDLE CENTREPIECE Ingredients

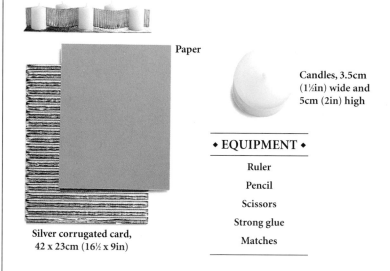

Paper

Candles, 3.5cm (1½in) wide and 5cm (2in) high

Silver corrugated card, 42 x 23cm (16½ x 9in)

◆ EQUIPMENT ◆

Ruler

Pencil

Scissors

Strong glue

Matches

FLOWER COLLAR Ingredients

Silver corrugated card

◆ EQUIPMENT ◆

Pencil

Ruler

Scalpel or craft knife

Metal ruler

Flower

Glass and water

REFLECTING LIGHT
Add even more sparkle with foil-wrapped almonds in frosted glass dishes and a candle centrepiece made with corrugated silver card.

MAKING THE CANDLE CENTREPIECE

This simple card centrepiece makes the most of the light from
five candles by reflecting it around the table. Make the central
divider as tall as the candles, which are short and wide to
minimize the risk of them toppling over.

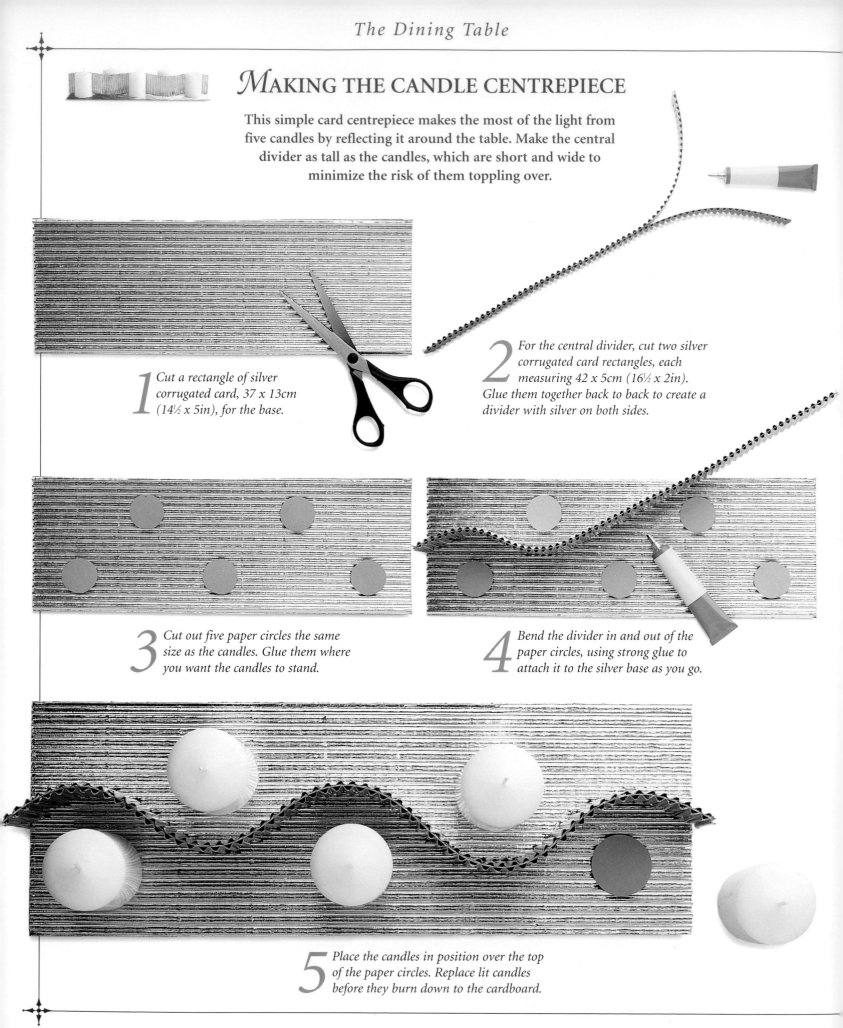

*1 Cut a rectangle of silver
corrugated card, 37 x 13cm
(14½ x 5in), for the base.*

*2 For the central divider, cut two silver
corrugated card rectangles, each
measuring 42 x 5cm (16½ x 2in).
Glue them together back to back to create a
divider with silver on both sides.*

*3 Cut out five paper circles the same
size as the candles. Glue them where
you want the candles to stand.*

*4 Bend the divider in and out of the
paper circles, using strong glue to
attach it to the silver base as you go.*

*5 Place the candles in position over the top
of the paper circles. Replace lit candles
before they burn down to the cardboard.*

MAKING THE FLOWER COLLAR

A star-shaped silver collar is the perfect backdrop for a
hot-pink flower. Choose a glass the right size for the flower
you wish to use, and ensure that you make the collar
large enough to cover the rim of the glass.

*1 Draw a star on the back of a piece of
silver corrugated card. Draw a circle the
size of the stem in the centre of the star.*

*2 Use a scalpel or craft knife and metal
ruler to cut out the star and the
small circle in the centre.*

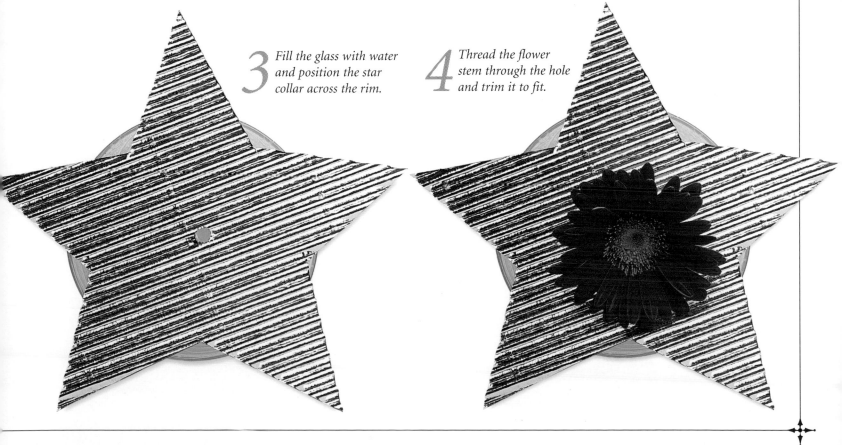

*3 Fill the glass with water
and position the star
collar across the rim.*

*4 Thread the flower
stem through the hole
and trim it to fit.*

TARTAN TABLE SETTING

THE TRADITIONAL TARTAN look in holly green and berry red makes a classic evening setting for a Christmas Day or Hogmanay feast. Soft chenille cloth, leaf-green plates in textured wood and smooth china, green-handled cutlery, linen napkins and chunky glass goblets are bathed in a rosy glow from two red candles, while home-made tartan crackers sit enticingly at each place setting.

FESTIVE CRACKERS Ingredients

One sheet patterned wrapping paper

Card, 25 x 25cm (10 x 10in)

Gift

Paper hat

117cm (46in) ribbon

Snap

◆ EQUIPMENT ◆

Pencil

Ruler

Scissors

Sticky tape

Glue

Brown card

String

Star name tag

LEAVES AND BERRIES
Continue the festive colour scheme with a circular centrepiece of garden evergreens and glossy red and gold baubles on wire stems.

MAKING THE CRACKER

Large and luxurious home-made Christmas crackers in a festive tartan print are extra-special when filled with carefully chosen gifts. Select a strong wrapping paper that will hold its shape when gathered at the ends of the cracker.

1 Draw a rectangle 45 x 23.5cm (18 x 9¼in) on the wrapping paper and cut it out.

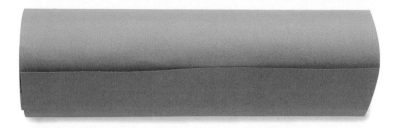

2 Cut a square 20 x 20cm (8 x 8in) out of the card and roll it into a tube, securing with tape.

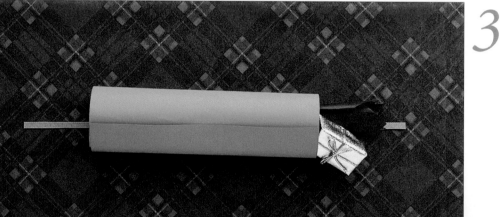

3 Place the wrapping paper face down and lay the card tube in the middle. Put the snap, gift and hat inside the tube.

4 Form the cracker by rolling the wrapping paper around the tube, then tape or glue to secure.

5 Roll a piece of brown card into a slightly tighter tube than the cracker and tape it. Carefully slide it into one end of the wrapping paper.

6 Wind a piece of string loosely around the cracker where the two tubes meet. Pull the string gently, and slowly push the brown tube in until a neat gather is made.

7 Replace the string with ribbon tied in a bow. Move the brown tube to the other end of the cracker and repeat step 6 at that end.

Shop-bought sparkly stars make excellent labels for personalized crackers

Take care not to tear the paper when tying the bows

8 Replace the final piece of string with a bow. To finish, make a matching bow and glue it to the middle of the cracker with a name tag.

CHRISTMAS FOOD

*Christmas would not be the same without
a celebration meal, complete with traditional
decorated cakes and biscuits, but why not sample
the specialities of another country for a change?
Try elegant French oyster tarts as a starter;
roast goose or venison instead of turkey; and
strudel or pavlova for a memorable Christmas
pudding. Non meat-eaters can enjoy splendid
dishes of salmon, trout and carp, while vegetarians
will be impressed by a spectacular delicacy
stuffed with wild mushrooms.*

STARTERS

BEGIN THE FESTIVE MEAL WITH A STARTER that balances and contrasts with the main dish to come. Choose from warming, hearty soups served with noodles or dumplings, delicate salads of smoked ham or marinated salmon, stylish oyster tarts or smoked salmon parcels. If you are short of time, nothing could be easier than a colourful plate of prosciutto with figs and melon or spicy boudin blanc pâté, prepared in advance: either will give an elegant, exotic feel to your Christmas dinner.

◆ BOUDIN BLANC PATE ◆

INGREDIENTS
butter, for greasing
375g (12oz) belly of pork, chopped
250g (8oz) chicken breast, chopped
2 onions, chopped
2 garlic cloves
60g (2oz) fresh white bread
4 tbsp white wine
2 eggs (size 3)
150ml (¼ pint) single cream
salt and black pepper
1 tsp ground mace
4 red dessert apples
2 tbsp lemon juice
ground allspice
red pepper strips and watercress sprigs, to garnish

ILLUSTRATED BELOW
BOUDIN BLANC IS THE FRENCH VERSION OF WHITE PUDDING. IT IS MADE WITH WHITE MEAT SUCH AS PORK AND CHICKEN, WELL FLAVOURED WITH GARLIC AND SPICES, THEN SHAPED INTO A SAUSAGE OR COOKED AS INDIVIDUAL PATES.

SERVES 6

1 Preheat the oven to 180°C/350°F/gas 4. Lightly butter 6 individual ramekin dishes.

2 Place the pork, chicken breast, onion, garlic and bread in a food processor. Blend until smooth. Add the wine, eggs, cream, salt, pepper and mace. Blend again until the mixture is smooth.

3 Fill the ramekins with the mixture, and smooth the tops. Cover the tops with foil and stand the ramekins in a roasting tin. Pour in enough boiling water to come two-thirds of the way up the sides of the dishes.

4 Bake the pâtés for 50–60 minutes until firm to the touch. Remove the dishes from the tin, discard the foil, and leave to cool.

5 Meanwhile, core and thinly slice the apples. Sprinkle with lemon juice and allspice, place on a baking sheet lined with foil and bake for 20 minutes. Cool.

6 Turn out the pâtés on to individual plates and garnish with thin strips of red pepper and sprigs of watercress. Serve with the apple slices and toast.

Smoked salmon parcels
(see page 148)

Boudin blanc pâté

Gravlax Salad

Ingredients
2 tbsp sea salt
1 tbsp caster sugar
2 tsp coarsely ground black pepper
30g (1oz) fresh dill, finely chopped
1kg (2lb) salmon fillets
cooked beetroot, lamb's lettuce and fresh dill sprigs

MUSTARD SAUCE
2 tbsp Dijon mustard
1 tbsp white wine vinegar
1 tbsp caster sugar
60ml (4 tbsp) olive oil
1 tbsp chopped fresh dill

ILLUSTRATED ON PAGE 172
THIS NORWEGIAN SPECIALITY HAS A
DELICATE, PEPPERY FLAVOUR.

SERVES 6

1 Mix the salt, sugar and pepper in a bowl. Sprinkle a layer of the mixture over the base of a shallow glass dish. Sprinkle on some of the chopped dill and lay one salmon fillet on top, skin-side down.

2 Sprinkle the fillet with more salt mixture and dill, then cover with a second fillet, skin-side up, arranging them head to tail.

3 Repeat with the remaining fillets, ensuring they are layered skin next to skin and flesh next to flesh. Cover the dish with clingfilm, place a board or plate on top and weigh down with a few weights. Leave for 2–3 hours at room temperature, then refrigerate for 3–4 days, turning the fillets daily.

4 To make the mustard sauce, whisk the ingredients in a bowl until well blended.

5 Drain the salmon fillets, slice thinly and arrange on a serving dish with strips of beetroot, lamb's lettuce and dill sprigs. Serve with the mustard sauce.

Prosciutto with Figs & Melon

Ingredients
1 small galia melon
6 fresh figs, quartered
6 slices prosciutto, cut into thin strips
fresh mint sprigs and lime slices, to garnish

DRESSING
4 tbsp melon juice
4 tbsp olive oil
2 tsp freshly squeezed lime juice
1 tsp clear honey
1 tsp herb mustard
salt and black pepper

ILLUSTRATED BELOW
PROSCIUTTO, ALSO KNOWN AS PARMA HAM, IS
A TRADITIONAL ITALIAN HAM WHICH HAS BEEN
DRY CURED, AND MATURED FOR ONE YEAR.
SLICED VERY THINLY AND SERVED WITH FRESH
FIGS AND SWEET MELON IT MAKES A LIGHT,
FESTIVE STARTER THAT IS VERY QUICK
AND EASY TO PUT TOGETHER.

SERVES 6

1 Halve and deseed the melon. Scoop the flesh into small balls using a melon baller.

2 Arrange the melon balls, fig quarters and strips of prosciutto on individual plates.

3 Pour the melon juice into a bowl with the oil, lime juice, honey, mustard, salt and pepper and whisk until well blended.

4 Pour some dressing over each serving and garnish with mint sprigs and a lime slice.

Christmas Eve soup
(see page 149)

Tomato & red pepper soup
(see page 149)

Prosciutto with figs & melon

Smoked Salmon Parcels

INGREDIENTS

8 slices smoked salmon
200g (7oz) cream cheese
2 hard-boiled eggs, chopped
1 tsp herb mustard
salt and black pepper
6 sun-dried tomatoes, drained and chopped
2 tbsp chopped fresh chives
fresh chive stems, salad leaves and
lemon wedges, to garnish

ILLUSTRATED ON PAGE 146
SCOTLAND HAS ALWAYS PRODUCED SALMON WITH A SUPERIOR FLAVOUR. TRY THESE DELICIOUS SMOKED SALMON PARCELS AS AN ELEGANT AND UNUSUAL STARTER.

MAKES 8

1 Trim each of the smoked salmon slices into 8 neat squares. Chop the remaining salmon trimmings finely.

2 Place the cheese, eggs, mustard, salt and pepper in a bowl and beat until smooth. Stir in the tomatoes, chopped chives and chopped salmon until evenly blended.

3 Place some filling in the centre of each salmon square and fold the salmon over the filling to make a neat parcel.

4 Tie chive stems around each parcel to secure, and place on a plate garnished with salad leaves and lemon wedges.

Festive Oyster Tarts

INGREDIENTS

125g (4oz) plain flour, plus extra for flouring
salt and black pepper
90g (3oz) butter, cut into small pieces
1 egg yolk
12 oysters, well scrubbed
1 tbsp olive oil
2 shallots, finely chopped
1 garlic clove, crushed
1 tbsp chopped fresh dill
1 tbsp chopped fresh tarragon
1 egg
150ml (¼ pint) single cream
black pepper
salad leaves and fresh tarragon, to garnish

ILLUSTRATED ON PAGE 152
OYSTERS ARE A TYPICAL STARTER TO A FRENCH CHRISTMAS LUNCH OR DINNER.

MAKES 12

1 To make the pastry, sift the flour, salt and pepper into a bowl. Add the butter and rub in finely with the fingertips. Mix in the egg yolk with a fork to form a firm dough, adding a little cold water if necessary. Knead on a lightly floured surface until smooth.

2 Roll out the pastry thinly and use to line 12 fluted tart tins measuring 7cm (3in). Trim off the excess pastry and press the pastry into the tins. Chill for 30 minutes. Preheat the oven to 200°C/400°F/gas 6.

3 Bake the pastry shells for 5–10 minutes until the pastry is lightly browned at the edges. Reduce the oven temperature to 190°C/375°F/gas 5.

4 Open the oysters using an oyster knife. Place the oysters and their juices in a bowl.

5 Heat the oil in a frying pan and cook the shallots, garlic, dill and tarragon for 1–2 minutes until tender. Add the oysters, reserving the juices, and cook for 1 minute.

6 Divide the mixture between the pastry cases. Beat the oyster juices with the egg, cream and pepper and add to the pastry cases. Return to the oven for 10–15 minutes until the filling has set. Serve garnished with salad leaves and fresh tarragon.

Beef Soup with Noodles

INGREDIENTS

2 tbsp vegetable oil
1kg (2lb) small beef bones
500g (1lb) piece shin of beef
2 chicken portions (or a chicken carcass)
1 large onion, quartered
2 carrots, peeled and quartered
1 leek, sliced
4 celery sticks, sliced
1 fresh bay leaf
½ tsp black peppercorns
½ tsp allspice berries
salt
3.5 litres (6 pints) cold water
chopped fresh parsley
NOODLES
125g (4oz) plain flour, plus extra for flouring
½ tsp salt
1 egg

ILLUSTRATED ON PAGE 166
THIS RICH, MEATY SOUP IS OFTEN SERVED ON CHRISTMAS DAY IN GERMANY, FOLLOWED BY ROAST GOOSE, HARE OR VENISON.

SERVES 6

1 Heat the oil in a large pan. Add the bones, beef and chicken and brown evenly. Alternatively, bake in a preheated oven at 200°C/400°F/gas 6 for 20 minutes, or until evenly browned, then transfer to a pan.

2 Add the vegetables, bay leaf, peppercorns, allspice, salt and water to the pan. Bring to the boil, cover and simmer for 3 hours.

3 Meanwhile, make the noodles. Sieve the flour and salt into a bowl. Add the egg and mix together, adding enough water to make a firm dough.

4 Knead the dough on a lightly floured surface until smooth, then wrap in clingfilm until required.

5 Strain the stock into a bowl and allow to cool. Skim off the fat, return the stock to the pan and bring to the boil.

6 Roll the dough out thinly on a lightly floured surface. Cut the dough into shapes using a small star cutter. Drop the shapes directly into the soup and return to the boil. The noodles are cooked when they rise to the surface. Divide the noodles equally between individual plates and serve the soup hot, sprinkled with chopped parsley.

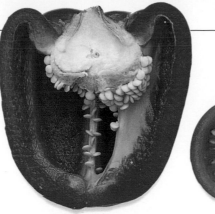

Tomato & Red Pepper Soup

INGREDIENTS

3 red peppers, halved, cored and deseeded

1kg (2lb) ripe tomatoes, halved and deseeded

2 red onions, quartered

2 garlic cloves, peeled

2 tbsp tomato purée

1.25 litres (2 pints) vegetable stock

salt and black pepper

3 tbsp single cream

*croûtons, cut from a slice of bread with a holly
leaf cutter and fried in butter, to garnish*

ILLUSTRATED ON PAGE 147

ROASTED SWEET RED PEPPERS GIVE THIS SOUP
ITS INTENSE FLAVOUR AND FESTIVE COLOUR.

SERVES 6

1 Preheat the oven to 200°C/400°F/gas 6. Place the peppers, tomatoes, onion and garlic in a roasting tin and bake in the oven for 15–20 minutes until the pepper skins have blistered.

2 Allow to cool slightly, then remove the skins from the peppers, tomatoes and onions and place in a food processor with the garlic, tomato purée and 150ml (¼ pint) of the vegetable stock.

3 Blend the vegetable mixture until smooth, then pour into a large pan and add the remaining stock, salt and pepper. Bring to the boil and simmer for 15 minutes.

4 Taste the soup and season if necessary. Serve in individual soup bowls with a swirl of cream and garnish with a few holly leaf croûtons.

Christmas Eve Soup

INGREDIENTS

MUSHROOM STOCK

*90g (3oz) dried mushrooms, or
250g (8oz) fresh mushrooms, chopped*

1 fresh bay leaf

900ml (1½ pints) boiling water

BEETROOT STOCK

*1kg (2lb) small beetroot, peeled and
chopped or grated*

1 litre (1¾ pints) cold water

150ml (¼ pint) red wine

½ tsp salt

black pepper

fresh rosemary sprigs, to garnish

DUMPLINGS

60g (2oz) butter

1 onion, finely chopped

1 tsp chopped fresh marjoram

1 tbsp fresh white breadcrumbs

salt and black pepper

125g (4oz) plain flour

1 tsp salt

1 egg

2–3 tsp cold water

ILLUSTRATED ON PAGE 147

CHRISTMAS EVE IN POLAND IS A FAST DAY,
WHEN NO MEAT IS SERVED, BUT THERE IS
PLENTY TO EAT, INCLUDING SOUP, NOODLES,
FISH AND PASTRIES. THIS BEETROOT SOUP
IS SERVED WITH STUFFED NOODLES
KNOWN AS "LITTLE EARS".

SERVES 6

1 Place the mushrooms and bay leaf in a pan with the water. Leave for 2 hours to soak if the mushrooms are dried.

2 Bring to the boil and simmer uncovered for 45–50 minutes until the liquid has reduced to 150ml (¼ pint). Strain the stock through a sieve into a bowl, pressing through all the liquid, and reserve the mushrooms.

3 Meanwhile, place the beetroot and water in a stainless steel pan and bring to the boil. Cover and simmer for 30 minutes, or until the beetroot is tender. Add the wine, salt and pepper and cook for another 10 minutes. Strain the beetroot stock through a fine sieve into a bowl, pressing through all the juices. Discard the beetroot.

4 To make the dumplings, melt the butter and fry the onion until tender. Stir in the marjoram and the reserved mushrooms and cook until all the liquid has evaporated.

Remove from the heat and stir in the breadcrumbs. Taste, season and allow to cool.

5 Sift the flour into a bowl, add the salt, egg and enough water to bind the mixture together, then knead into a soft dough.

6 Roll out the dough on a lightly floured surface to a paper-thin square and cut into about 60 x 3.5cm (1½in) squares. Cover with a damp tea-towel to prevent the dough from drying out. Knead the trimmings together, roll out, and again cut into squares.

7 Place a teaspoon of the mushroom filling in the centre of each square and keep covered with a damp tea-towel. Taking one square at a time, fold in half diagonally and seal the edges. Take the two points at the base of the triangle and pinch together. Place on a floured plate. Repeat with the remaining squares to make about 70 dumplings.

8 Cook a few dumplings at a time in a large pan of boiling salted water for 5 minutes. Remove with a slotted spoon and drain on paper towels. Place on a warm plate, cover with foil and keep warm.

9 Pour the beetroot and mushroom stocks into a pan and bring to the boil. Taste for seasoning. Arrange a few dumplings in each warm bowl and ladle the soup over them. Garnish with rosemary sprigs.

MAIN DISHES

EVERY COUNTRY HAS ITS OWN CHRISTMAS TRADITIONS, especially when it comes to food. Britain and America are devoted to turkey, but in other countries fish and game are equally popular. Celebration dishes that have survived in Europe since medieval times include roast goose, baked carp and roast venison. Some, such as the salt cod of Provence, were eaten as a fasting dish on Christmas Eve. Vegetarians, too, are well catered for – try the impressive herbed nut roulade, encased in golden filo pastry, or a tall loaf of Russian bread, stuffed with wild mushrooms and soft cheese.

❖ HERBED NUT ROULADE ❖

INGREDIENTS
200g (7oz) packet filo pastry
90g (3oz) melted butter
beaten egg, to glaze
clementine shells filled with cranberry sauce
(see page 158) and blueberries, and
fresh rosemary sprigs, to garnish

NUT MIXTURE
2 tbsp vegetable oil
2 onions, finely chopped
2 tbsp chopped fresh parsley
250g (8oz) brazil nuts, finely chopped
250g (8oz) whole peeled chestnuts, finely chopped
250g (8oz) fresh wholemeal breadcrumbs
grated zest and juice of 1 orange
salt and black pepper
2 eggs (size 3)

VEGETABLE FILLING
2 red peppers, halved, cored and deseeded
2 yellow peppers, halved, cored and deseeded
1 tbsp vegetable oil
375g (12oz) courgettes, thinly sliced
2 tbsp chopped fresh oregano

THIS MOIST, FLAVOURSOME NUT MIXTURE WITH ROASTED PEPPERS AND COURGETTES IS WRAPPED IN CRISP LAYERS OF FILO PASTRY. IT MAKES AN IDEAL CELEBRATION DISH FOR VEGETARIANS, HOT OR COLD.

SERVES 6–8

1 Preheat the oven to 200°C/400°F/gas 6. To make the nut mixture, heat the oil in a pan, add the onion and cook gently for 2–3 minutes until soft. Place in a large bowl. Add the parsley, nuts, breadcrumbs, orange zest and juice, salt and black pepper. Mix together until well blended. Stir in the eggs and mix together to form a ball. Allow to cool.

2 To make the vegetable filling, place the pepper halves on a baking sheet, skin uppermost, and roast for 10–15 minutes until the skin has charred and bubbled. Allow to cool, then carefully peel off the skin.

3 Heat the oil in a pan and add the courgette slices and oregano. Cook gently for 2–3 minutes until tender, stirring occasionally, then allow to cool.

4 Line a baking sheet with non-stick baking parchment. Spread the nut mixture over the paper into an oblong measuring approximately 30 x 25cm (12 x 10in).

5 Spread the vegetables evenly over the nut mixture and roll up from the long edge into a neat roll with the help of the paper.

6 Line another baking sheet with non-stick baking parchment. Take 3 sheets of filo pastry, keeping the remainder covered with a damp tea towel, and lay them over the baking sheet, overlapping slightly. Brush with melted butter and cover with another 3 sheets. Repeat until you have used 12 sheets of pastry.

7 Place the nut roll down the centre of the pastry, with the join underneath. Bring one of the long sides of the pastry layers over the roll. Fold in the ends and bring the remaining side of the pastry over to cover neatly. Brush the pastry with melted butter.

8 Fold the remaining pastry in two, cut out leaf shapes and decorate the top. Bake for 20–30 minutes, covering the top with baking parchment when it becomes light brown.

9 Cool slightly, then slide the roulade on to a warmed serving dish. Garnish with clementine shells filled with cranberry sauce and blueberries, and with rosemary sprigs.

Baked Aubergines with Feta & Herbs

Ingredients

3 aubergines, halved lengthways
2 red peppers, halved, cored and deseeded
2 courgettes, halved lengthways
1 onion, quartered
2 garlic cloves, crushed
375g (12oz) tomatoes, halved
3 tbsp olive oil
salt and black pepper
1 tbsp each chopped fresh parsley,
basil and oregano
60g (2oz) fresh white breadcrumbs
1 egg
200g (7oz) feta cheese, sliced
fresh herb sprigs, to garnish

THE DARK, SHINY SKINS OF
AUBERGINES ENCASE MOIST LAYERS OF
VEGETABLES, HERBS AND FETA CHEESE.

SERVES 6

1 Preheat the oven to 200°C/400°F/gas 6. Arrange the aubergines, peppers, courgettes, onion, garlic and tomatoes on a baking sheet and sprinkle with 2 tablespoons of oil, salt and pepper. Bake in the oven for 15–20 minutes until tender. Remove from the oven and reduce the heat to 180°C/350°F/gas 4.

2 Scoop out the aubergine flesh, keeping the skins intact, and reserve the shells. Peel the peppers and peel and deseed the tomatoes. Chop the vegetables finely and mix well in a bowl with the herbs, breadcrumbs and egg.

3 Brush a 1.5 litre (2½ pint) mould with the remaining oil. Line the base and sides with the aubergine shells, placing the dark skin side against the mould.

4 Lay one-third of the feta cheese slices over the base of the mould and cover with one-third of the vegetable mixture. Repeat with alternate layers of cheese and vegetables until the mould is completely filled.

5 Cover the top with foil. Stand the mould in a large roasting tin and pour in enough hot water to come two-thirds of the way up the side of the mould.

6 Bake in the oven for 45 minutes until the filling has set. Leave to cool in the mould for 15 minutes, then turn out on to a warm serving dish. Garnish with herb sprigs.

Mushroom Bread

Ingredients

YEAST DOUGH
500g (1lb) plain strong white flour, plus
extra for flouring
1 tsp salt
2 sachets easy-blend dried yeast
175ml (6fl oz) warm milk
2 eggs, beaten
125g (4oz) unsalted butter, softened, plus extra
melted butter for brushing
1 egg yolk
1 tbsp water
FILLING
2 tbsp olive oil
1 garlic clove, crushed
2 shallots, sliced
500g (1lb) wild or assorted mushrooms, trimmed
1 tbsp chopped fresh parsley
1 tbsp chopped fresh coriander
salt and black pepper
1 tbsp plain flour
150ml (¼ pint) white wine
500g (1lb) low-fat curd or soft cheese

FOR CENTURIES THE UKRAINE HAS BEEN
KNOWN AS THE "BREAD BASKET OF EUROPE"
BECAUSE ITS FERTILE SOIL PRODUCES AN
ABUNDANCE OF GRAIN. THE REGION HAS
MANY DIFFERENT WAYS OF MAKING BREAD,
AND A DIFFERENT-SHAPED BREAD FOR
EVERY CONCEIVABLE OCCASION.

SERVES 6

1 Sift the flour and salt into a mixing bowl and add the yeast, milk and eggs. Mix with a wooden spoon to form a soft dough, then beat for 5–8 minutes until the mixture is smooth, glossy and elastic. Alternatively, place in a food mixer or processor fitted with a dough beater and work for 2–3 minutes.

2 Beat the butter in a bowl until light and fluffy. Gradually add the butter to the dough, beating well after each addition until all the butter has been incorporated and the dough is smooth and glossy. If using a mixer, set at low speed.

3 Cover the bowl with clingfilm and leave in a warm place to rise for 1–2 hours, or until the dough has doubled in size. Brush a 23cm (9in) sandwich tin with melted butter. To make the glaze, beat the egg yolk and water together.

4 Meanwhile, make the filling. Heat the oil in a frying pan, add the garlic and shallots and cook until tender. Add the mushrooms and fry quickly for 3 minutes. Stir in the herbs, salt and pepper.

5 Stir the flour and wine into the pan, bring to the boil and cook for 1 minute. Remove from the heat and leave until cold.

6 Knead the dough into a smooth ball on a lightly floured surface and roll out to a 40cm (16in) circle. Place the dough in the tin, and press it across the base and up the sides, allowing the excess to drape over the sides.

7 Spread half the cheese over the base, cover with the mushroom filling, then add the remaining cheese. Draw the excess dough over the filling in deep pleats, rotating the tin and pleating the dough evenly. Draw the ends together and twist them into a small knob.

8 Preheat the oven to 200°C/400°F/gas 6. Cover the tin and leave in a warm place for about 20 minutes, or until the dough has risen and puffed up again.

9 Brush the loaf with the glaze and bake for 45–50 minutes, until well risen and golden brown. Turn the loaf out and leave it to cool on a wire rack for 10 minutes. Serve the bread hot, cut into slices.

CHRISTMAS EVE IN PROVENCE

THIS IS THE *GROS SOUPER* OF PROVENCE, served on Christmas Eve. It actually forms part of a fast, so fish is served, not meat, but it is still a sumptuous feast. The meal ends with the "Thirteen Desserts", symbolizing Christ and the twelve Apostles. The centrepiece is a rich olive bread, surrounded by an assortment of fruit and nuts.

Festive Oyster Tarts p.148 & top left

Salt Cod Provençal p.154 & centre
Chard au Gratin p.164 & bottom left

The Thirteen Desserts
p.181 & top right

Salt Cod Provençal

INGREDIENTS
750g (1½lb) salt cod
15g (½oz) plain flour
black pepper
2 tbsp olive oil
30g (1oz) butter
fresh herb sprig, to garnish
PROVENÇAL SAUCE
1 large onion, sliced
2 garlic cloves, crushed
750g (1½lb) tomatoes, skinned and chopped
1 tbsp tomato purée
1 tbsp capers
1 tbsp gherkins
1 tbsp each chopped fresh tarragon,
thyme and parsley

ILLUSTRATED ON PAGES *152–53*
SALT COD MUST BE CAREFULLY PREPARED
TO BRING OUT ITS DELICATE FLAVOUR. AT
CHRISTMAS, PROVENÇAL MARKETS
HAVE SPECIAL STALLS SELLING READY-
PREPARED SALT COD.

SERVES 6

1 Soak the cod in plenty of cold water, in a cool place, for 24 hours, changing the water 3–4 times.

2 Drain the fish and pat dry with kitchen paper. Cut into 6 even-sized pieces, discarding the fins and bones. Season the flour with black pepper. Dip the fish pieces in the flour until evenly coated on both sides.

3 Heat the oil and butter in a large frying pan. Add half the pieces of fish and fry until golden brown on both sides. Remove the fish with a slotted spoon and drain on kitchen paper. Keep warm while the remaining pieces of fish are cooked.

4 To make the Provençal sauce, add the onion and garlic to the pan and cook for 2–3 minutes until tender but not browned. Stir in the tomatoes and tomato purée and bring to the boil. Cook gently for 2–3 minutes, then stir in the capers, gherkins and herbs and season with black pepper.

5 Pour the sauce on to a large warm serving dish and carefully arrange the fish on top. Garnish with a sprig of fresh herbs.

Poached Salmon with Hollandaise Sauce

INGREDIENTS
2.75kg (6lb) whole salmon, cleaned
2–3 sprigs of fresh dill
2 fresh bay leaves
4 shallots, quartered
1 tbsp black peppercorns
1 tbsp salt
¼ cucumber, thinly sliced
1 lemon, thinly sliced
fresh dill sprigs, to garnish
HOLLANDAISE SAUCE
8 egg yolks (size 3)
90ml (3fl oz) lemon juice
salt and black pepper
375g (12oz) unsalted butter
1 bunch watercress (optional)
1 bunch fresh basil (optional)

A WONDERFUL CENTREPIECE FOR A
CHRISTMAS BUFFET, THIS POPULAR SALMON
DISH IS EASY TO PREPARE. FOR EXTRA
COLOUR, SERVE WITH A GREEN
HOLLANDAISE SAUCE.

SERVES 10–12

1 Wash the salmon, dry with kitchen paper and place the dill sprigs in the cavity. Arrange the salmon in a fish kettle or large roasting tin. Add the bay leaves, shallots, peppercorns and salt, and pour in enough water to cover the salmon. Cover with non-stick baking parchment, and then with the fish kettle lid or foil.

2 Bring slowly to the boil on top of the stove, then turn off the heat and leave to stand for 30 minutes. If the salmon is to be served cold, allow to stand until the water is completely cold.

3 Meanwhile, make the hollandaise sauce. Place the egg yolks, lemon juice, salt and pepper in a blender or food processor and blend until smooth.

4 Heat the butter gently in a pan until it is bubbling, but do not allow it to brown. With the machine running, slowly add half the melted butter to the egg yolk mixture in a steady stream. Blend for about 10 seconds until it is well incorporated.

5 Add the remaining butter in a steady stream and continue to blend until the mixture is pale and has thickened. Taste for seasoning, then pour the sauce into a warm sauce boat or bowl. Keep warm in a bain marie, or over a pan of warm water.

6 To make green hollandaise, strip the leaves from the watercress. Add the watercress leaves and basil to the sauce in the blender when all the butter has been added. Process until smooth.

7 Drain off the liquid from the fish kettle. Carefully lift out the salmon, place on a large serving dish and keep warm. Cut the skin neatly round the head and tail and carefully peel off the skin, including the fins, leaving the head and tail intact.

8 Arrange overlapping cucumber slices along the backbone of the salmon, and alternate lemon and cucumber slices around the head. Garnish with sprigs of dill and serve with the hollandaise sauce.

CARP WITH SWEET & SOUR SAUCE

INGREDIENTS

2kg (4lb) carp, cleaned and descaled
30g (1oz) unsalted butter
2 carrots, chopped
1 leek, sliced
4 celery sticks, sliced
2 onions, quartered
2 bay leaves
2 sprigs of fresh thyme
1 tsp allspice berries
2 strips of lemon zest
salt and black pepper
1.2 litres (2 pints) water
600ml (1 pint) brown ale
60g (2oz) raisins
60g (2oz) ginger spiced cake or biscuits
chopped fresh parsley, lemon wedges and
toasted flaked almonds, to garnish

THIS GERMAN RECIPE DATES FROM THE MIDDLE AGES, WHEN MONASTERIES HAD SPECIAL FISHPONDS FOR BREEDING CARP. THEY WOULD START TO FATTEN THE FISH FOR CHRISTMAS ON ST BARTHOLOMEW'S DAY (AUGUST 24).

SERVES 6

1 Wash the carp and dry on kitchen paper. Melt the butter in a large ovenproof dish or casserole, add the carrots, leek, celery and onion and cook for 4–5 minutes until the vegetables have softened, stirring occasionally. Add the bay leaves, thyme, allspice berries, lemon zest, salt and pepper.

2 Arrange the fish on top of the bed of vegetables and pour over the water and brown ale. Bring to the boil on top of the stove, then cover and cook very gently over a low heat for 15–20 minutes, or until the fin pulls out easily.

3 Remove the fish carefully, using two fish slices, and place on a warm serving dish. Keep warm while you make the sauce.

4 Strain the stock from the vegetables into a pan. Add the raisins. Crumble the cake or biscuits and stir the crumbs into the pan. Bring to the boil and simmer for 1 minute until slightly thickened. Spoon the sauce over the fish and garnish with chopped parsley, lemon wedges and toasted flaked almonds.

TROUT WITH DARK FRUIT SAUCE

INGREDIENTS

30g (1oz) unsalted butter
6 trout, cleaned and trimmed
salt and black pepper
finely grated zest of 1 lemon
2 tbsp chopped fresh parsley
SAUCE
60g (2oz) caster sugar
600ml (1 pint) water
4 tbsp red wine vinegar
2 fresh bay leaves
2 tbsp blackcurrant jelly
60g (2oz) pitted prunes, chopped
60g (2oz) dried apricots, chopped
grated zest and juice of 1 lemon
lemon wedges and fresh parsley sprigs, to garnish

THIS FISH RECIPE WITH ITS UNUSUAL SAUCE COMES FROM THE CZECH REPUBLIC. THE CONTRAST OF THE BRIGHT PINK TROUT AGAINST THE DARK FRUIT SAUCE MAKES A VERY APPEALING DISH.

SERVES 6

1 Melt the butter in a shallow flameproof dish. Sprinkle the trout with salt, pepper, lemon zest and parsley, then add to the dish and fry for a few minutes on each side to brown evenly.

2 To make the sauce, place the sugar and 1 tablespoon of the water in a pan. Heat gently until the sugar dissolves, then boil rapidly until the syrup turns a rich brown.

3 Add the vinegar to the syrup and stir to dissolve the caramel. Stir in the remaining water, bay leaves, blackcurrant jelly, prunes, apricots, lemon zest and juice. Bring the sauce to the boil and pour over the trout in the flameproof dish. Cover and cook gently for 5 minutes until the fish is tender.

4 Lift out the trout on to a board and carefully remove the skin, leaving the head and tail intact. Arrange the trout on a serving dish and keep warm.

5 Bring the sauce to the boil and cook until it has reduced and thickened. Serve the trout on individual plates and spoon the sauce around. Garnish with lemon wedges and parsley sprigs.

DIP-IN-THE-POT CRUSTED HAM

INGREDIENTS

3-4kg (6-8lb) knuckle end salt-cured ham
2 large onions, sliced
2 carrots, sliced
1 leek, sliced
4 celery sticks, sliced
2 fresh bay leaves
½ tsp peppercorns
4 cloves
600ml (1 pint) lager
2 x 250g (8oz) smoked pork sausages
rye bread, to serve

CRUST

250g (8oz) rye or wholemeal flour
500g (1lb) fresh white breadcrumbs
125g (4oz) soft brown sugar
30g (1oz) each chopped fresh parsley and dill
2 tbsp dry mustard
2 eggs, beaten
90ml (6 tbsp) clear honey
2 tbsp finely chopped fresh parsley

THE SWEDISH RITUAL KNOWN AS "DIPPING IN THE POT" DATES BACK TO THE TIME WHEN NOTHING COULD BE WASTED, AND BROTH LEFT OVER FROM COOKING THE CHRISTMAS HAM WAS NO EXCEPTION. EVERYONE DIPS A PIECE OF RYE BREAD INTO THE BROTH.

SERVES 6–8

1 Soak the ham in cold water for 12 hours, changing the water 2–3 times. Drain well.

2 Place the ham in a large pan, cover with water and bring to the boil. Remove the ham and pour off the water.

3 Place the onions, carrots, leek, celery, bay leaves, peppercorns and cloves in the pan. Add the ham, lager and sausages and enough water to cover. Bring to the boil, cover and cook very gently for 2 hours. Leave the ham and sausages to cool overnight in the broth.

4 To make the crust, mix the flour, breadcrumbs, sugar, parsley, dill and mustard in a bowl until evenly blended. Mix in just enough of the beaten egg to bind the mixture together.

5 Preheat the oven to 200°C/400°F/gas 6. Remove the ham from the broth and drain well. Peel off the skin and score the fat with a sharp knife. Warm the honey and brush evenly over the ham.

6 Press the crumb mixture over the ham until evenly covered. Place the ham in a roasting tin and bake for 40–50 minutes or until the crust is golden brown. Allow to cool.

7 Remove the sausages from the broth. Strain the broth through a sieve, pushing through the vegetables with a wooden spoon. Return the broth to the pan and bring to the boil. Adjust the seasoning and sprinkle with chopped parsley.

8 Arrange the ham on a serving dish with the sausages. Serve with the broth, and a plate of rye bread cubes for dipping.

ROAST VENISON WITH APPLES & PEARS

INGREDIENTS

2–3kg (4–6 lb) short saddle of venison
2 tbsp olive oil
60g (2oz) butter
2 onions, sliced
1 leek, sliced
4 celery sticks, sliced
60g (2oz) plain flour
125g (4oz) bacon fat, cut into strips
4 dessert pears, halved and cored
4 red apples, halved and cored
juice of 2 lemons
2 tsp clear honey
4 tbsp brandy
150ml (¼ pint) sour cream
sprigs of fresh rosemary, to garnish

MARINADE

600ml (1 pint) dry red wine
600ml (1 pint) cold water
1 tsp each whole cloves, peppercorns and juniper berries
1 fresh bay leaf
2 tsp salt

DEER ARE STILL HUNTED IN THE FORESTS OF GERMANY DURING THE SEASON. AFTERWARDS, THE SPOILS ARE HONOURED WITH A TORCHLIT CEREMONY AND A SPECIAL SALUTE FROM THE HUNTING HORNS.

SERVES 6–8

1 To make the marinade, place the wine, water, cloves, peppercorns, juniper berries, bay leaf and salt in a stainless steel pan. Bring the marinade to the boil, then leave to cool to room temperature.

2 Place the venison in a large dish or stainless steel roasting tin. Pour over the marinade, cover and leave at room temperature for 6 hours, turning frequently, or in the refrigerator for 2 days.

3 Preheat the oven to 180°C/350°F/gas 4. Pour the oil into a roasting tin and heat in the oven until very hot.

4 Remove the venison, reserving the marinade, and pat the meat dry with kitchen paper. Add to the roasting tin and brown on all sides, turning frequently.

5 Meanwhile, melt the butter in a large pan and add the onion, leek and celery. Cook quickly, stirring occasionally, until the vegetables are lightly browned.

6 Add the flour and cook over a low heat, stirring until golden brown, taking care not to burn the flour. Stir in the marinade, bring to the boil and remove from the heat.

7 Remove the venison from the roasting tin, pour in the vegetable mixture and place the venison on top. Cover with the strips of bacon fat. Roast in the oven for 1½ hours, basting with the marinade, until the meat is tender and slightly pink.

8 Meanwhile, slice the pear and apple halves thinly, but not all the way through, keeping the fruit intact. Place each piece of fruit on a square of foil, pour over the lemon juice and drizzle each with honey. Seal the parcels, place on a baking sheet and bake in the oven for 5–10 minutes until tender.

9 Place the venison on a warm serving dish and remove the strips of bacon fat. Strain the marinade and vegetables through a fine sieve, pressing out all the juices. Bring to the boil, add the brandy and cream, taste and season. Pour some of the sauce around the venison and serve the remainder in a warm sauce boat. Garnish the venison with the pear and apple halves, and sprigs of rosemary.

STANDING RIBS OF BEEF WITH A MUSTARD CRUST

INGREDIENTS
3kg (6lb) forerib of beef, chined (6 bone)
MUSTARD CRUST
2 tbsp oil
175g (6oz) fresh breadcrumbs
1 onion, finely chopped
2 tbsp chopped fresh oregano
1 tbsp mixed peppercorns, crushed
½ tsp salt
4 tbsp English wholegrain mustard

THE ROAST BEEF OF OLD ENGLAND REMAINS A CHERISHED NATIONAL DISH. ORIGINALLY, LARGE JOINTS OF BEEF WERE SPIT-ROASTED OVER AN OPEN FIRE, AND YORKSHIRE PUDDINGS WERE COOKED UNDERNEATH IN THE BEEF JUICES. IN THIS RECIPE THE BEEF IS GIVEN A CRISP COATING TO KEEP THE MEAT MOIST AND FULL OF FLAVOUR.

SERVES 6

1 Preheat the oven to 220°C/425°F/gas 7. To make the mustard crust, stir the oil, breadcrumbs, onion, oregano, peppercorns and salt in a bowl until evenly mixed. Add the mustard to the bowl and stir until the mixture begins to bind together.

2 Press the mixture evenly over the flesh side of the ribs, leaving the bones uncovered. Place the ribs of beef in a roasting tin with the mustard crust side uppermost.

3 Roast the beef in the oven for 30 minutes, then reduce the heat to 190°C/375°F/gas 5 and cook for another hour, or until the meat is cooked to your taste, allowing 20 minutes per 500g (1lb) for rare beef, 25-30 minutes for medium, and 30-35 minutes for well-done. Cover the crust with foil if it becomes too brown.

4 Transfer the meat to a warm serving dish and leave to firm up for 15 minutes, making it easier to carve.

5 Cut into slices to serve – the crust will crumble as it is sliced. Serve a little crust with each portion and accompany the beef with Yorkshire puddings, roast potatoes and vegetables such as Brussels sprouts.

ROAST LAMB

INGREDIENTS
3–3.5kg (6–7lb) leg of lamb
5 garlic bulbs
sprigs of fresh rosemary, thyme and parsley
salt and black pepper
2 tbsp clear honey
1 tbsp lemon juice
lemon wedges and fresh parsley sprigs,
to garnish

ILLUSTRATED ON PAGE 173
THIS CELEBRATION ROAST FROM NORWAY SHOWS A DEFINITE FRENCH INFLUENCE, WITH THE FLAVOURS OF ROASTED GARLIC AND HERBS.

SERVES 6

1 Preheat the oven to 190°C/375°F/gas 5. Place the leg of lamb in a roasting tin. Divide one garlic bulb into cloves, and peel and slice the cloves.

2 Using a sharp knife, make small incisions all over the lamb. Insert alternate sprigs of herbs and slivers of garlic until the lamb is evenly covered.

3 Roast the lamb in the oven for 1¾ hours, then remove and brush with the honey and lemon juice. Return the lamb to the tin with the remaining garlic bulbs. Roast for another 30–40 minutes until the lamb is tender and slightly pink inside.

4 Arrange on a serving dish and garnish with lemon wedges, parsley sprigs and the bulbs of garlic, divided into cloves.

STUFFED QUAIL WITH GRAPES

INGREDIENTS

8 oven-ready quails
4 tbsp olive oil
salt and black pepper
500g (1lb) red or white seedless grapes
250ml (½ pint) chicken stock
vine leaves, to garnish (optional)

STUFFING

30g (1oz) butter
2 shallots, chopped
1 garlic clove, crushed
4 chicken livers, chopped
60g (2oz) sun-dried tomatoes, chopped
2 tbsp chopped fennel
salt and black pepper
3 tbsp Marsala
60g (2oz) fresh white breadcrumbs

AN ELEGANT RECIPE FROM TUSCANY,
SUITABLE FOR PIGEONS AS WELL AS QUAIL.

SERVES 4–6

1 To make the stuffing, melt the butter in a frying pan, add the shallots and garlic and cook for 1–2 minutes until tender. Add the livers and fry for a few minutes.

2 Add the sun-dried tomatoes, fennel, salt, pepper and Marsala. Bring to the boil and remove from the heat. Stir in the fresh breadcrumbs and leave to cool.

3 Place a quail on a board, breast-side down, and remove the backbone by cutting down each side with kitchen scissors. Turn the bird over and flatten by pressing down on the breastbone with the heel of your hand. Repeat with the remaining quails.

4 Preheat the oven to 190°C/375°F/gas 5. Loosen the skin of the quails from the flesh with your fingers and spoon the stuffing beneath the skin. Spread the stuffing evenly over the flesh of the quails and pull the skin tight to flatten it. Hold the legs and wings in place with cocktail sticks and arrange the quails in a large roasting tin. Brush the skins with olive oil and season.

5 Place two-thirds of the grapes in a food processor and blend until smooth. Strain the grape mixture through a sieve and pour over the quails with the stock.

6 Roast the quails in the preheated oven for 30–40 minutes until tender, covering with foil if they brown too quickly.

7 To serve, arrange the quails on a warmed serving dish, strain the sauce and pour over. Garnish with small bunches of the remaining grapes and a few vine leaves, if available. Serve with Glazed Florentine Fennel (see page 163).

ROAST GOOSE WITH APPLE & NUT STUFFING

INGREDIENTS

4–5kg (8-10lb) oven-ready goose with giblets
salt and black pepper
6 slices goose or bacon fat
3 red dessert apples, halved and cored
3 green dessert apples, halved and cored
juice of 1 lemon
2 tbsp clear honey
125g (4oz) toasted almonds, to garnish
fresh rosemary sprigs, to garnish

STUFFING

60g (2oz) butter
175g (6oz) raisins
4 onions, chopped
3 cooking apples, peeled, cored and coarsely chopped
125g (4oz) blanched almonds, chopped
250g (8oz) fresh white breadcrumbs
1 tbsp each chopped fresh parsley, sage and thyme
1 tsp ground cloves

ILLUSTRATED ON PAGES 166-67
GOOSE STUFFED WITH APPLES AND NUTS IS
THE TRADITIONAL CHRISTMAS DAY BIRD IN
GERMANY. THE USUAL ACCOMPANIMENTS ARE
RED CABBAGE AND POTATO DUMPLINGS.

SERVES 6–8

1 Preheat the oven to 200°C/400°F/gas 6. Wipe the goose and remove any excess fat from inside. Place the giblets in a pan with water to cover, and season. Bring to the boil, cover and simmer for 45 minutes. Reserve the stock for gravy. Chop the liver for stuffing.

2 To make the stuffing, melt the butter and cook the raisins, onion and apple for 2–3 minutes, stirring. Remove from the heat and add the almonds, breadcrumbs, herbs, cloves and chopped liver.

3 Stuff the neck end of the goose, securing the skin flap underneath the wing tips, and place the remainder in the body cavity of the goose or make stuffing balls. Secure the tail end with skewers, and truss the goose neatly with string to hold the wings and legs in position, close to the body.

4 Cover the breast with goose or bacon fat and tie on securely with string. Sprinkle with salt and pepper. Place a rack in a large roasting tin and lay the goose breast-side down. Cook in the oven for 30 minutes, then reduce the heat to 180°C/ 350°F/gas 4.

5 Remove the goose from the oven and prick the skin around the neck, wings, thighs, back and lower breast. Return to the oven for another 3–3½ hours, removing excess fat and basting regularly. Add stuffing balls 30 minutes from the end of the cooking time.

6 Test the goose by piercing the thigh with a sharp knife – the juices should run pale yellow, not pink. Leave the goose to rest for 15 minutes before carving.

7 Meanwhile, slice the apple halves thinly, but not all the way through. Place each half on a square of foil, drizzle with lemon juice and honey, and add a sprig of rosemary. Seal the parcels and bake in the oven for 10–15 minutes, then unwrap carefully.

8 Place the goose on a warm serving dish and garnish with the apples, stuffing balls, toasted almonds and sprigs of rosemary.

Roast Turkey with Cornbread Stuffing

INGREDIENTS
5.5kg (12lb) oven-ready turkey
500g (1lb) streaky bacon
5–6 clementine shells filled with cranberries
and blueberries, slices of spiced, buttered
pumpkin, roasted chestnuts and sage sprigs,
to garnish

CORNBREAD STUFFING
30g (1oz) butter
3 onions, finely chopped
2 garlic cloves, chopped
6 celery sticks, chopped
250g (8oz) pork sausagemeat
2 x 240g (8½oz) can whole peeled chestnuts,
finely chopped
250g (8oz) cornbread, crumbled
1 tbsp each chopped fresh parsley, sage
and thyme
salt and black pepper
1 tsp ground cinnamon
zest and juice of 1 orange
1 egg (size 3)

ILLUSTRATED ON PAGES *160-61*
ROAST TURKEY IS POPULAR IN BOTH BRITAIN AND AMERICA AT CHRISTMAS. CORNBREAD IS USUALLY THE FAVOURITE AMERICAN STUFFING.

SERVES 6–8

1 To make the stuffing, melt the butter in a pan, add the onion, garlic and celery and cook for 2 minutes, stirring occasionally. Add the sausagemeat and cook quickly until lightly brown. Remove the pan from the heat.

2 In a bowl mix together the chestnuts, cornbread, parsley, sage, thyme, salt, pepper, cinnamon, orange zest and juice. Add the sausagemeat mixture. Stir until evenly blended, then mix in the egg.

3 Place one-quarter of the stuffing in the neck end of the turkey, pull over the skin flap and secure under the turkey using a trussing needle and string.

4 Fill the cavity of the turkey with the remaining stuffing, pull the skin over the tail and secure with the needle and string. Alternatively, make small stuffing balls.

5 Truss the turkey, using the needle and string to secure the wings and legs close to the body, and place in a roasting tin. Cover with bacon rashers to keep the meat moist while cooking. Chill until ready to cook.

6 Preheat the oven to 190°C/375°C/gas 5. Roast the turkey for 2 hours, then remove the bacon and cover with foil.

7 Return the turkey to the oven for a further 2 hours. Add stuffing balls 30 minutes before the end. To test for doneness, pierce with a sharp knife between the legs and body of the turkey – the juices should run clear.

8 Leave the turkey to stand for 20 minutes before removing the trussing string. Place on a warm serving dish and garnish with clementine shells filled with cranberries and blueberries, stuffing balls, if using, slices of spiced, buttered pumpkin, roasted chestnuts and sage sprigs.

Plum, Lemon & Herb Stuffing

INGREDIENTS
30g (1oz) butter
2 onions, finely chopped
500g (1lb) plums, halved,
stoned and sliced
grated zest and juice of 1 large lemon
1 tbsp clear honey
1 tbsp each chopped fresh thyme,
oregano and parsley
1 tsp salt
½ tsp freshly ground black pepper
250g (8oz) medium oatmeal
375g (12oz) fresh white breadcrumbs
2 eggs (size 3), beaten

THIS LIGHT, TANGY STUFFING IS ENOUGH TO STUFF A 5.5KG (12LB) TURKEY. IF FRESH PLUMS ARE UNAVAILABLE USE 500G (1LB) OF CANNED PLUMS, WELL DRAINED.

1 Melt the butter in a medium-sized pan, add the onion and plums and cook gently for 5 minutes until almost tender. Stir in the lemon zest and juice, the honey, herbs, salt and pepper.

2 Mix the oatmeal and breadcrumbs in a large bowl, and add the onion mixture and eggs. Stir until evenly blended, then cover and chill until ready to use.

Chestnut & Cranberry Stuffing

INGREDIENTS
30g (1oz) butter
2 onions, finely chopped
250g (8oz) cranberries
1 tsp ground cinnamon
grated zest and juice of 1 orange
2 x 240g (8½oz) cans whole, peeled chestnuts,
finely chopped
250g (8oz) fresh white breadcrumbs
salt and black pepper
1 egg (size 3)

A STUFFING WITH A NUTTY FLAVOUR AND TEXTURE; MAKES ENOUGH TO STUFF A 5.5KG (12LB) TURKEY.

1 Melt the butter in a medium-sized pan, add the onion and cook gently for 2 minutes. Add the cranberries, cinnamon, orange zest and juice and cook gently for 2 minutes. Remove from the heat.

2 Place the chopped chestnuts, breadcrumbs, salt and pepper in a large bowl and mix well. Stir in the cranberry and orange mixture and the egg, and mix until well blended. Cover the stuffing with clingfilm and chill until ready to use.

AMERICAN CHRISTMAS LUNCH

SINCE THE DAYS OF THE EARLY AMERICAN SETTLERS roast turkey has been served as a celebration dish. Cornbread stuffing and a sweet-sour cranberry sauce are the usual accompaniments, other favourites being mashed potatoes flavoured with garlic and herbs, stuffed onions and creamed spinach. Desserts special to the Americans include crunchy pecan pie, rich, sweet and dark, and a creamy, tangy cheesecake topped with fresh blueberries.

Roast Turkey p.159 & centre
Cranberry Sauce p.165 & top
Stuffed Onions p.164 & top left
Garlic & Herb Potatoes p.162
& bottom left
Creamed Spinach p.164 & bottom right

.

Pecan Pie p.171 & top right
Blueberry Cheesecake p.171 & centre right

ACCOMPANIMENTS

ROAST POTATOES AND BRUSSELS SPROUTS are often served with the Christmas meal, but there are plenty of alternatives to excite a jaded palate. Try the garlicky mashed potatoes served with the American turkey, or wickedly rich gratin potatoes, cooked with cream, Gruyère cheese and egg.

Chard, the spinach-like vegetable beloved by the French, would make an exciting change, cooked au gratin, as would glazed Florentine fennel, flavoured with pine nuts, garlic and ginger. Even humble Brussels sprouts take on a new lease of life when tossed with toasted almonds, thyme and lemon.

◆ POTATO DUMPLINGS ◆

INGREDIENTS
1kg (2lb) medium-sized potatoes, scrubbed
salt and black pepper
30g (1oz) plain flour
30g (1oz) semolina
1½ tsp freshly ground nutmeg
2 eggs, beaten
2 tbsp toasted breadcrumbs

THESE LIGHT, FLUFFY DUMPLINGS ARE ONE OF THE TRADITIONAL ACCOMPANIMENTS FOR ROAST GOOSE.

MAKES 12

1 Boil the potatoes in salted water for about 10 minutes, until almost tender. Drain, leave until cool enough to handle, then peel.

2 Mix together in a bowl the flour, semolina, salt, pepper and nutmeg.

3 Grate the potatoes coarsely and add to the bowl. Mix in lightly.

4 Add the eggs and mix together to form a soft dough, adding more flour if necessary. Using floured hands, shape the mixture into 20 round balls.

5 Cook the dumplings in boiling salted water for 8-10 minutes, or until they rise to the surface. Remove with a slotted spoon and drain on kitchen paper.

6 Arrange the dumplings on a warm serving plate and sprinkle with toasted breadcrumbs, or roll them individually in the breadcrumbs to coat evenly.

◆ SWISS FRIED POTATOES ◆

INGREDIENTS
8 medium-sized baking potatoes
salt and black pepper
1 tbsp chopped fresh parsley
3 tbsp olive oil
30g (1oz) butter
sprigs of fresh parsley, to garnish

OTHERWISE KNOWN AS RÖSTI, THESE GOLDEN BROWN POTATO CAKES ARE A SWISS SPECIALITY.

SERVES 6

1 Boil the potatoes in salted water for about 10 minutes, until almost tender. Drain, leave until cool enough to handle, then peel. Place the cooked potatoes in a bowl, cover and chill for 1 hour.

2 Grate the potatoes on a coarse grater into a bowl. Add pepper and the chopped parsley and mix together.

3 Heat the oil and butter in a non-stick frying pan. Place heaped tablespoonfuls of the potato mixture in the pan, evenly spaced apart. Press the potatoes into flat shapes using a fish slice, and cook for 2-3 minutes until golden brown underneath.

4 Turn each potato cake once, and cook for another 2-3 minutes to brown the other side. Remove with a fish slice and keep warm while cooking the remaining mixture. Arrange on a warm serving plate and garnish with sprigs of parsley.

◆ GARLIC & HERB POTATOES ◆

INGREDIENTS
1.5kg (3lb) potatoes, peeled and cut into chunks
6 garlic cloves, peeled
salt and black pepper
60g (2oz) butter
60ml (2 fl oz) milk
2 tbsp chopped fresh parsley

ILLUSTRATED ON PAGE 160
IN AMERICA, SMOOTH, CREAMY, GARLIC-FLAVOURED POTATOES ARE OFTEN SERVED WITH THE CHRISTMAS TURKEY.

SERVES 6

1 Bring the potatoes and garlic to the boil in salted water. Cover and simmer gently for 10 minutes, or until the potatoes are tender.

2 Drain the potatoes and garlic, add pepper, butter and milk, and mash until smooth and creamy. Stir in the parsley and pile on to a warm serving dish. Serve with roast turkey.

GRATIN POTATOES

INGREDIENTS
60g (2oz) butter
1kg (2lb) potatoes, peeled
salt and black pepper
grated nutmeg
175g (6oz) Gruyère, grated
150ml (¼ pint) single cream or milk
1 egg (size 3)

ILLUSTRATED ON PAGE *172*
THIS CREAMY POTATO DISH MAKES THE
PERFECT ACCOMPANIMENT TO A LARGE JOINT,
SUCH AS ROAST BEEF OR LAMB.

SERVES 6

1 Preheat the oven to 190°C/375°F/gas 5. Lightly butter a shallow, ovenproof dish.
2 Using a large grater or the slicer on a food processor, slice the potatoes thinly.

3 Arrange a layer of potato slices in the dish and sprinkle with salt, pepper, nutmeg and a little grated cheese. Continue to layer the potatoes and cheese, reserving a little cheese for the top, until the dish is filled. Beat together the cream and egg and pour over the top of the dish.
4 Sprinkle the top with the reserved cheese. Bake for 40–50 minutes, or until the top is golden brown and the potato is tender.

CARAMELIZED CARROTS & ONIONS

INGREDIENTS
24 baby carrots, peeled
24 pickling onions
125g (4oz) caster sugar
4 tbsp water
125g (4oz) unsalted butter
1 tbsp lemon juice
1 tbsp chopped fresh parsley

ILLUSTRATED ON PAGE *173*
CARAMELIZED VEGETABLES ACCOMPANY THE
CHRISTMAS ROAST DINNER IN NORWAY.

SERVES 6

1 Place the carrots and onions in separate pans of boiling salted water. Cover and simmer for 5–10 minutes, until tender. Drain and cool slightly, then peel the onions.
2 Gently heat the sugar and water, stirring occasionally, until the sugar has dissolved.

3 Boil rapidly until the bubbles subside and a golden-brown syrup forms. Add the butter and stir to blend evenly, then stir in the lemon juice until smooth.
4 Place the carrots and onions in the caramel and toss to coat evenly. Place on a warm serving plate and sprinkle with chopped parsley. Serve hot.

GLAZED FLORENTINE FENNEL

INGREDIENTS
150ml (¼ pint) vegetable stock
3 fennel bulbs, quartered
1 tbsp olive oil
30g (1oz) unsalted butter
2 tbsp pine nuts
2 red onions, cut into wedges
2 garlic cloves, sliced
1cm (½ in) root ginger, peeled and cut into strips

A WONDERFUL MIXTURE OF COLOURS
AND FLAVOURS IS REFLECTED IN
THIS ITALIAN RECIPE.

SERVES 6

1 Place the stock in a pan and bring to the boil. Add the fennel quarters and cook for 2 minutes. Remove using a slotted spoon and keep warm. Reserve the stock.

2 Heat the oil and butter in a frying pan, add the pine nuts and brown lightly. Remove with a slotted spoon.
3 Add the onion, garlic, ginger and fennel quarters to the pan. Cook for 1-2 minutes, turning the vegetables gently. Pour in the stock and cook quickly for 1 minute. Arrange the fennel and onions in a serving dish and sprinkle with the pine nuts.

Stuffed Onions

Ingredients

6 medium-sized white onions, peeled
2 tbsp olive oil
1 garlic clove, crushed
250g (8oz) wild mushrooms, chopped
2 tbsp chopped fresh oregano
salt and black pepper
2 tbsp fresh white breadcrumbs
150ml (¼ pint) vegetable stock
2 tbsp dry sherry
fresh parsley sprigs, to garnish

ILLUSTRATED ON PAGE 160
TRY THE MILD, SWEET FLAVOUR OF WHITE
ONIONS, FILLED WITH A MIXTURE OF WILD
MUSHROOMS AND HERBS.

SERVES 6

1 Preheat the oven to 200°C/400°F/gas 6. Place the onions in a pan of boiling water for 5 minutes, then drain well and cool.

2 Scoop out the centre of each onion, leaving the base and shell intact. Chop the centres finely.

3 Heat the oil in a frying pan and quickly cook the chopped onion, garlic and mushrooms for 1–2 minutes until tender. Stir in the oregano, salt, pepper and breadcrumbs.

4 Fill the cavity of each onion with the mushroom mixture. Place the remaining stuffing in an ovenproof dish and arrange the onions on top.

5 Pour the stock and sherry into the dish and bake for 30 minutes or until the onions are tender. Arrange on a warm serving dish and garnish with parsley sprigs.

Creamed Spinach

Ingredients

1.5kg (3lb) spinach
SAUCE
30g (1oz) butter
30g (1oz) plain flour
salt and black pepper
150ml (¼ pint) milk
½ tsp freshly grated nutmeg
2 tbsp double cream

ILLUSTRATED ON PAGE 161
FRESHLY COOKED SPINACH IS SERVED WITH A
CREAMY SAUCE FLAVOURED WITH NUTMEG.

SERVES 6

1 Cook the spinach in 150ml (¼ pint) boiling water for 1 minute, then drain well and chop finely.

2 To make the sauce, place the butter, flour, salt, pepper and milk in a small pan.

Whisk continuously over a moderate heat until the sauce thickens.

3 Simmer the sauce over a low heat for 2 minutes, stirring occasionally. Add the nutmeg and spinach and stir until well blended and heated through.

4 Add the cream, stir well and pour into a warm serving dish.

Chard au Gratin

Ingredients

1kg (2lb) chard, trimmed
2 tbsp olive oil
1 garlic clove, crushed
30g (1oz) plain flour
150ml (¼ pint) vegetable stock
150ml (¼ pint) white wine
salt and black pepper
½ tsp freshly grated nutmeg
1 tbsp black pitted olives, halved
60g (2oz) Gruyère cheese, grated
2 tbsp fresh white breadcrumbs

ILLUSTRATED ON PAGE 152
THIS WONDERFUL LEAFY GREEN VEGETABLE
IS A FAVOURITE WITH THE FRENCH.

SERVES 6

1 Slice the chard into bite-sized lengths. Heat the oil in a large frying pan.

2 Add the garlic and chard and fry quickly for 1 minute, stirring all the time. Remove the chard with a slotted spoon and set aside.

3 Stir in the flour, stock, wine, salt, pepper and nutmeg. Bring to the boil and cook

for 2 minutes. Add the chard and olives and stir to mix well.

4 Put the chard mixture into a flameproof dish and sprinkle with the cheese and breadcrumbs. Place under a hot grill until lightly browned and bubbling.

Brussels Sprouts with Almonds

Ingredients

750g (1½lb) Brussels sprouts
salt and black pepper
30g (1oz) butter
60g (2oz) flaked almonds
1 tbsp chopped fresh thyme
2 tsp lemon zest

THE TRADITIONAL ENGLISH VEGETABLE
WHICH IS IN SEASON AT CHRISTMAS. TO MAKE
THE SPROUTS MORE APPEALING, TOSS THEM
WITH ALMONDS, THYME AND LEMON.

SERVES 6

1 Quarter the Brussels sprouts if large, otherwise cut them in half. Fill a large pan one-third full of salted water and bring to the

boil. Add the sprouts, cover and simmer for 5 minutes until they are just tender and bright green. Drain well.

2 Meanwhile, melt the butter in a frying pan, add the almonds and stir-fry until they are golden brown.

3 Stir in the thyme, lemon zest and pepper, add the sprouts and toss well to coat evenly. Place in a warm serving dish.

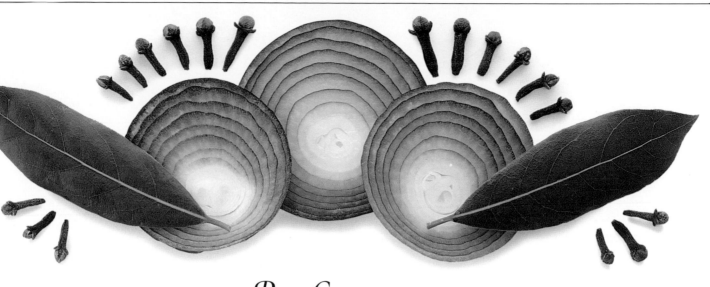

Red Cabbage

Ingredients

1 red cabbage, finely shredded
150ml (¼ pint) red wine vinegar
30g (1oz) caster sugar
1 tsp salt
4 whole cloves
1 fresh bay leaf
30g (1oz) goose fat or 2 tbsp vegetable oil
2 red onions, sliced
1 cooking apple, peeled, cored and sliced
150ml (¼ pint) giblet stock
4 tbsp redcurrant jelly
150ml (¼ pint) red wine

ILLUSTRATED ON PAGE 166
SPICY SWEET AND SOUR RED CABBAGE IS A
FAVOURITE WINTER DISH ALL OVER EUROPE. IT
IS A TRADITIONAL ACCOMPANIMENT TO ROAST
GOOSE, AND IS OFTEN COOKED IN GOOSE FAT.

SERVES 6

1 Place the cabbage, vinegar, sugar, salt, cloves and bay leaf in a bowl and mix to blend evenly.

2 Heat the goose fat or oil in a flameproof casserole, add the onions and apple and cook until lightly browned, stirring.

3 Stir in the cabbage and stock and bring to the boil. Cover and cook gently for about 30 minutes until the cabbage is tender and most of the stock has evaporated. Add more stock or water if necessary.

4 Just before serving, stir in the redcurrant jelly and wine.

Cucumber, Dill & Sour Cream Salad

Ingredients

2 cucumbers, peeled
1 tsp salt
150ml (¼ pint) crème fraîche
1 tbsp white wine vinegar
½ tsp caster sugar
black pepper
1 tbsp chopped fresh dill

THIS LIGHT AND REFRESHINGLY TANGY
SALAD COMES FROM AUSTRIA.

SERVES 6

1 Cut the cucumbers in half lengthways. Scoop out the seeds and cut crosswise into thin slices. Spread the slices over a large dish and sprinkle with salt. Cover and leave at room temperature for 15 minutes.

2 Meanwhile, mix the crème fraîche, vinegar, sugar and pepper in a bowl.

3 Place the cucumber slices in a nylon sieve and press out the liquid. Pat dry on kitchen paper then add to the crème fraîche mixture and turn gently to coat evenly.

4 Cover the cucumber salad and chill until required. Place in a serving dish and sprinkle with dill.

Cranberry Sauce

Ingredients

250ml (8 fl oz) water
125g (4oz) caster sugar
4 tbsp redcurrant jelly
500g (1lb) cranberries
zest and juice of 1 orange
125g (4oz) walnuts, chopped (optional)

ILLUSTRATED ON PAGE 161
CRANBERRIES ARE ALWAYS SERVED WITH
ROAST TURKEY IN AMERICA. ADD CHOPPED
NUTS FOR EXTRA TEXTURE.

SERVES 6

1 Gently heat the water, caster sugar and redcurrant jelly in a pan, stirring occasionally, until the sugar has dissolved.

2 Add the cranberries and bring to the boil. Simmer uncovered for 15 minutes. Stir in the orange zest and juice, and the walnuts, if using. Leave to cool.

3 Place in a serving dish, cover and chill until required.

A German Christmas Dinner

This hearty spread is reminiscent of medieval banquets. A rich, warming soup is followed by roast goose stuffed with apples and nuts, a popular feast dish that is served with red cabbage and potato dumplings. The apples and nuts are highly symbolic: apples represent the tree of knowledge, while nuts stand for the mystery of life. A spectacular coiled strudel makes a splendid dessert, followed by stollen, the fruit-filled bread always baked for Christmas.

Beef Soup with Noodles p.148 & left

·

Roast Goose with Apple Stuffing
p.158 & centre
Potato Dumplings p.162 & bottom right
Red Cabbage p.165 & centre

·

Celebration Strudel p.170 & centre right
Stollen p.180 & top right

DESSERTS

THIS RICH ASSORTMENT OF DESSERTS will delight the eye as well as the palate. For a truly spectacular presentation, choose a dramatic coiled strudel filled with soft cheese and spices, or a Christmas pudding shaped like a fruity cannonball and crowned with a sprig of holly. For a lighter touch, try the Italian zuccotto, a delicious confection of cream, chocolate and nuts encased in coffee-flavoured sponge fingers, or a delicate vanilla-flavoured cream, shaped in a ring mould and filled with colourful fruit and leaves. And for sheer self-indulgence, sherry trifle is hard to beat.

ENGLISH CHRISTMAS PUDDING

INGREDIENTS
375g (12oz) mixed dried fruit
200g (7oz) dried fruit salad (apples, apricots, mangoes etc.), chopped
60g (2oz) flaked almonds
1 small carrot, coarsely grated
1 small cooking apple, coarsely grated
grated zest and juice of 1 lemon
1 tbsp black treacle
90ml (3fl oz) stout
60g (2oz) fresh white breadcrumbs
60g (2oz) plain flour
1 tsp ground allspice
60g (2oz) dark soft brown sugar
60g (2oz) butter, melted
1 egg (size 3)

BY TRADITION THE CHRISTMAS PUDDING IS MADE ON "STIR UP SUNDAY" – THE FIRST SUNDAY BEFORE ADVENT. THE WHOLE FAMILY USED TO GATHER TOGETHER TO STIR THE PUDDING MIXTURE IN A CLOCKWISE DIRECTION AND MAKE A WISH. IT WAS BELIEVED THAT STIRRING ANTI-CLOCKWISE WOULD STIR UP TROUBLE. THIS PUDDING WILL KEEP FOR A YEAR IF WRAPPED SECURELY AND STORED IN A COOL PLACE.

SERVES 6

1 Lightly butter a 15cm (6in) Christmas pudding mould and place a round of non-stick baking parchment in the bottom of each half of the mould.

2 Mix the dried fruit, almonds, carrot and apple in a large bowl. Stir in the lemon zest and juice, treacle and stout until well blended. Cover with clingfilm and leave in a cool place for a few hours, or overnight.

3 Add the breadcrumbs, sifted flour, allspice, sugar, butter and egg to the mixture. Mix together and stir well until thoroughly blended. Have ready a pan into which the pudding mould will fit comfortably.

4 Spoon the mixture into both halves of the mould so they are evenly filled. At this stage, you can insert silver coins or keepsakes, wrapped several times in greaseproof paper.

5 Place the two halves of the mould together, stand on the base and fasten the clip firmly to keep the pudding secure. Carefully place the mould in the pan.

6 Half-fill the pan with boiling water, making sure the level of the water is not above the join of the mould. Bring to the boil, cover and simmer very gently for 5–6 hours. Top up the pan with boiling water from time to time as required.

7 Remove from the pan and leave the pudding to cool in the mould. Carefully remove half the mould and leave until the pudding is completely cold. Turn out, wrap in clingfilm or foil, and store in a cool place until required. Reheat before serving.

8 To reheat, remove the clingfilm or foil, replace the Christmas pudding in the mould and cook for 1 hour in a pan of boiling water, as described above. Place on a heated serving dish and serve with Cumberland Rum Butter (see below).

CUMBERLAND RUM BUTTER

INGREDIENTS
90g (3oz) unsalted butter
90g (3oz) soft brown sugar
½ tsp freshly grated nutmeg
60ml (2fl oz) dark rum or brandy

CHRISTMAS PUDDING IS ALWAYS SERVED WITH A "HARD" SAUCE MADE OF CREAMED BUTTER, SUGAR AND RUM OR BRANDY. THE COMBINATION OF THE COLD, HARD SAUCE WITH THE HOT, SOFT FRUIT PUDDING IS TOO ENTICING TO RESIST.

SERVES 6

1 Place the butter in a bowl or food processor fitted with a metal blade. Beat or process the butter until white and creamy.

2 Add the sugar and nutmeg and beat again until light and fluffy.

3 Add the rum or brandy one drop at a time, beating continuously until enough has been added to flavour the butter well. Take care not to overbeat, as the mixture might then curdle.

4 Pile the rum butter into a dish, cover and leave in the refrigerator until firm. Serve a large spoonful with each serving of Christmas pudding.

TRADITIONAL SHERRY TRIFLE

INGREDIENTS

2 eggs, plus 2 yolks (size 3)
30g (1oz) caster sugar
1 tbsp cornflour
300ml (½ pint) milk
1 tsp vanilla essence
125g (4oz) Madeira cake, thinly sliced
2 tbsp strawberry or raspberry jam
2 tbsp Madeira wine
1 tbsp brandy
250g (8oz) strawberries or raspberries, halved
275ml (10fl oz) double cream
8 blanched almonds and strawberry leaves, to decorate (optional)

TRIFLE WAS VERY POPULAR IN VICTORIAN ENGLAND, WHERE IT WAS ALSO KNOWN AS "TIPSY" CAKE. IT IS EXTREMELY RICH.

SERVES 8

1 Whisk the whole eggs, yolks, sugar and cornflour in a bowl until well blended.

2 Place the milk in a pan with the vanilla essence and bring to the boil. Pour the milk on to the egg mixture in the bowl, whisking well.

3 Rinse the pan, then strain the custard through a sieve back into the clean pan. Cook over a gentle heat, whisking continuously, until it has thickened. Do not allow the custard to boil or it will curdle. Leave until cold.

4 Spread the Madeira cake slices with the jam and place a layer, jam-side down, in the base of a serving bowl. Mix together the Madeira wine and brandy and sprinkle over the cake slices. Repeat with the remaining cake slices and sprinkle over the remaining Madeira wine and brandy.

5 Cover the cake with two-thirds of the strawberry or raspberry halves. Place the cream in a bowl and whip until the cream stands in peaks.

6 Fold two-thirds of the cream into the cold custard until it is well blended and smooth. Spoon over the cake and fruit in the bowl and smooth the top.

7 Place the remaining whipped cream in a piping bag fitted with a small star nozzle. Pipe the cream over the top of the custard and decorate with blanched almonds, the remaining strawberries or raspberries and the leaves, if using. Chill until required.

ZUCCOTTO

INGREDIENTS

175g (6fl oz) coffee liqueur
20 sponge fingers
300ml (½ pint) double cream
30g (1oz) icing sugar, sifted
60g (2oz) pine nuts, toasted
60g (2oz) almonds, toasted and chopped
150g (5oz) plain chocolate dots
icing sugar and cocoa, to decorate

THIS DESSERT ORIGINATED IN FLORENCE – IT IS SAID THAT THE SHAPE RESEMBLES THE CUPOLA OF THE CATHEDRAL. ZUCCOTTO MEANS "LITTLE PUMPKIN", AND THE PUMPKIN-SHAPED MOULDS ARE ONLY OBTAINABLE IN ITALY, BUT A ROUND GLASS BOWL MAKES A GOOD SUBSTITUTE.

SERVES 6

1 Line the base and sides of a zuccotto mould, or a 1 litre (1½ pint) round-bottomed glass bowl with damp muslin, leaving the excess overlapping the sides.

2 Place 4 tablespoons of the coffee liqueur in a shallow dish. Dip one sponge finger at a time into the liqueur, then place lengthways down the side of the mould, sugared side against the muslin.

3 Repeat until the sides and bottom of the mould are completely lined, making sure there are no gaps and trimming the sponge fingers to fit tightly. Chill for 30 minutes. Reserve the remaining sponge fingers and any coffee liqueur remaining in the dish for the top of the mould.

4 Place the cream and icing sugar in a bowl and whisk until very thick. Spoon one-quarter of the cream into another bowl and mix in the nuts and 60g (2oz) of the chocolate dots until well blended.

5 Spread the cream and nut mixture carefully over the sponge fingers in an even layer, smoothing the surface. Chill.

6 Place the remaining chocolate dots and coffee liqueur in a heatproof bowl over a pan of hot water. Stir occasionally until melted. Leave to cool.

7 Add the remaining cream to the melted chocolate mixture and fold in carefully until evenly blended. Fill the centre of the mould with the chocolate cream and smooth the surface to make it level.

8 Cover the mould with the remaining sponge fingers and sprinkle with any remaining liqueur. Press down firmly. Bring the excess muslin over the top of the mould, place a plate on the surface and weight the top. Leave to chill overnight.

9 Remove the weights and plate and fold back the muslin. Invert the mould on to a serving plate and carefully remove the mould and the muslin. Dust the surface thickly with icing sugar, then dust alternate sections with cocoa using a wedge-shaped template.

Celebration Strudel

ILLUSTRATED ON PAGE 167

INGREDIENTS

90g (3oz) unsalted butter, melted
400g (13oz) cream cheese
3 eggs (size 3), separated
175g (6oz) caster sugar
175g (6oz) ground almonds
finely grated zest of 1 lemon
125g (4oz) sultanas
2 tsp ground cinnamon, plus extra for dusting
200g (7oz) filo pastry
icing sugar, for dusting

STRUDEL CAN BE MADE IN MANY DIFFERENT SHAPES AND SIZES, BUT THIS LARGE COIL IS ONE OF THE MOST SPECTACULAR, AND IDEAL FOR A SPECIAL OCCASION.

SERVES 6

1 Preheat the oven to 180°C/350°F/gas 4. Line a large baking tray with foil and brush with melted butter.

2 Place the cream cheese, egg yolks and half the sugar in a bowl. Mix together with a wooden spoon, then beat until smooth. Stir in the ground almonds, lemon zest, sultanas and cinnamon until evenly blended.

3 Whisk the egg whites in a clean bowl until stiff, then gradually add the remaining sugar, whisking well after each addition. Add to the cheese mixture and fold in gently until evenly mixed.

4 Brush one sheet of filo pastry with butter, keeping the remainder covered with a damp tea towel. Cover with a second sheet and brush again.

5 Spread 1 tablespoon of filling along the pastry 2.5cm (1in) in from the long edge. Roll the pastry over the filling into a long roll.

6 Arrange the roll in a spiral, starting at the centre of the baking tray. Repeat with the remaining filo pastry, butter and filling to make another 7 rolls, adding them on to the spiral to form a tight coil shape.

7 Brush the coil with melted butter and bake in the oven for 35–40 minutes until crisp and brown. Meanwhile, fold the remaining pastry in half and brush with melted butter. Cut out 6 holly leaves and bake for 2 minutes. Dust the coil with icing sugar and cinnamon and serve warm or cold, decorated with the holly leaves.

Fruit in Cognac

INGREDIENTS

250g (8oz) granulated sugar
300ml (½ pint) water
3 peaches
3 pears
3 clementines
30g (1oz) cranberries
brandy or liqueur

THIS MAKES A SPLENDID CHRISTMAS PRESENT, PACKED IN A DECORATIVE JAR. USE A COLOURFUL SELECTION OF FIRM, RIPE FRUIT.

SERVES 6

1 Place 125g (4oz) of the sugar and the water in a pan and heat gently, stirring occasionally until the sugar has dissolved.

2 Pour boiling water over the peaches, leave for 1 minute, then peel, halve, stone and cut into thin wedges. Peel, core and slice the pears. Peel the clementines and cut off the white pith with a sharp knife. Cut the clementines into thin slices.

3 Add all the fruit to the syrup, bring to the boil, then cook very gently for 8–10 minutes or until the fruit is tender.

4 Transfer the fruit to a heatproof dish, using a slotted spoon, and add the remaining sugar to the syrup in the saucepan. Heat the syrup, stirring occasionally, until the sugar has dissolved.

5 Boil rapidly until the temperature reaches 110°C/230°F on a sugar thermometer, or the thread stage is reached. Test by pressing a small amount of syrup between 2 teaspoons. When pulled apart, a thread should form.

6 When the syrup has cooled, pour into a measuring jug and add an equal quantity of brandy or liqueur. Pour over the fruit, cover and chill until required. If giving the fruit as a present, spoon into a sterilized jar and fill to the top with the syrup and liqueur. Secure with a screwtop lid.

Vanilla Cream Mould

ILLUSTRATED ON PAGE 173

INGREDIENTS

1 packet powdered gelatine
3 tbsp cold water
600ml (1 pint) double cream
2 tsp vanilla essence
30g (1oz) caster sugar
500g (1lb) assorted fruit, such as strawberries, raspberries, blueberries and cherries
strawberry leaves, to decorate (optional)

THIS DELICATE CREAM FROM NORWAY IS IDEAL TO FOLLOW A SUBSTANTIAL MAIN DISH.

SERVES 6

1 Place the gelatine and water in a small bowl over a pan of hot water and stir until the gelatine has dissolved.

2 Whisk the cream, vanilla essence and sugar until well blended. Add the dissolved gelatine and whisk until the mixture thickens. Pour the cream into a 900ml (1½ pint) 19cm (7½in) ring mould and leave in the refrigerator for 3–4 hours to set.

3 Dip the mould in hand-hot water and invert on to a serving dish. Fill the centre with mixed berries and arrange berries around the base of the mould. Decorate with strawberry leaves and serve with Berry Sauce (see opposite).

Berry Sauce

Ingredients

250g (8oz) raspberries
250g (8oz) strawberries
250g (8oz) blueberries
150ml (¼ pint) water
2 tsp arrowroot
4 tbsp cherry brandy

ILLUSTRATED ON PAGE 173
USE ANY ASSORTMENT OF FRESH SOFT
FRUIT IN SEASON.

SERVES 6

1 Place the berries and water in a pan and bring to the boil. Cover and simmer for 5 minutes. Pour into a food processor and blend until smooth, then sieve, or press the fruit and juice through a sieve into a bowl.

2 Place the purée in a pan and bring to the boil. Blend the arrowroot with a little water until smooth. Add to the purée, stirring continuously until it comes back to the boil.

3 Simmer for 2 minutes, cool and add the cherry brandy.

Blueberry Cheesecake

Ingredients

200g (7oz) plain flour, plus extra for flouring
150g (5oz) unsalted butter, cut into pieces
60g (2oz) caster sugar
1 egg yolk
FILLING
90g (3oz) caster sugar
500g (1lb) cream cheese
300ml (½ pint) sour cream
2 eggs (size 3)
1 tsp vanilla essence
finely grated zest of 1 orange
375g (12oz) blueberries
2 tbsp redcurrant jelly
icing sugar, to dust

ILLUSTRATED ON PAGE 161
THE MELT-IN-THE-MOUTH TEXTURE OF THE
SWEET PASTRY MAKES THIS AMERICAN
CHEESECAKE IRRESISTIBLE.

SERVES 6

1 Sift the flour into a bowl, add the butter and rub in finely with the fingertips until the mixture resembles breadcrumbs. Stir in the sugar and egg yolk and mix together to form a firm dough, adding a little cold water if necessary.

2 Roll out the dough on a lightly floured surface, thinly enough to line the base and sides of a 4.5cm (1¾in) deep, 21cm (8½in) loose-bottomed fluted flan tin. Trim the edge. Prick the base and chill for 30 minutes. Preheat the oven to 190°C/375°F/gas 5.

3 Line the pastry case with non-stick baking parchment and a thin layer of dried pulses, rice or ceramic baking beans. Bake blind in the preheated oven for 15 minutes, until the pastry is firm, but not brown. Remove the pastry from the oven and cool on a wire rack, still in the tin. Remove the paper and pulses, rice or beans, and reduce the heat to 150°C/300°F/gas 2.

4 For the filling, place the sugar, cream cheese, cream, eggs, vanilla and orange zest in a bowl and beat until smooth. Add one-third of the blueberries to the mixture. Fold them in gently until evenly mixed.

5 Pour the mixture into the pastry case and bake in the oven for 1 hour. Turn off the heat and allow the cheesecake to cool in the oven. When completely cool, release the tin and place the cheesecake on a serving plate.

6 Melt the redcurrant jelly in a small pan and brush the top of the cheesecake with the jelly. Arrange the remaining blueberries on top of the cheesecake and dust with icing sugar to serve.

Pecan Pie

Ingredients

150g (5oz) plain flour,
plus extra for flouring
¼ tsp salt
90g (3oz) butter, cut into pieces
3 tbsp cold water
corn syrup, to brush
FILLING
4 eggs (size 3)
250ml (8fl oz) corn, golden or maple syrup
90g (3oz) unsalted butter, melted
1 tsp vanilla essence
250g (8oz) pecan nuts

ILLUSTRATED ON PAGE 161
THE RICH, NUTTY FLAVOUR OF THIS PIE HAS
MADE IT A CLASSIC IN THE AMERICAN SOUTH.

SERVES 8–10

1 Sift the flour and salt into a bowl, add the butter and rub in with the fingertips until it resembles breadcrumbs. Stir in the water and mix to a firm dough with a fork.

2 Knead the dough on a lightly floured surface until smooth. Roll out and line the base and sides of a 23cm (9in) pie dish. Trim the edge, re-roll the trimmings and cut out 12 maple leaves with a leaf cutter. Brush the leaves with water and position around the rim of the pie. Chill for 15 minutes. Preheat the oven to 200°C/400°F/ gas 6.

3 Line the pastry case with non-stick baking parchment and bake blind (see above) for 10 minutes. Remove the paper and beans and cool. Reduce the heat to 180°C/ 350°F/gas 4.

4 To make the filling, whisk the eggs then slowly add the syrup, whisking to blend well. Whisk in the butter and vanilla and stir in the pecan nuts. Pour into the pastry case.

5 Bake for 40–45 minutes until risen, golden brown and set in the centre. Allow to cool, then brush with corn syrup to serve.

NORWEGIAN CHRISTMAS BUFFET

In Norway, the emphasis is on fresh, healthy ingredients, even at Christmas. The country's clear mountain streams produce some of the best fish in the world – hence the popularity of gravlax, the famous cured salmon. Tender lamb, bred on the high pastures, is cooked French-style on special occasions, with garlic and herbs, and the favourite dessert, a moulded cream, is filled with seasonal berries, the preferred choice being the rare Arctic cloudberry.

CAKES & BISCUITS

CHRISTMAS IS THE TIME FOR CELEBRATION CAKES. Rich, dark fruit cakes, redolent of wine and spices, are made well in advance and left to mature. Later, they can be covered with marzipan and lavishly iced. Fruit breads such as panettone, gingerbread and other spiced cakes are also traditional fare.

Macaroon cake, a fairy castle made of meringue, or festive pavlova, piled high with frosted fruit, would make a stunning centrepiece. Shaped biscuits, decorated with icing and tied with ribbons, can be hung on the tree to delight the children, while the grown-ups feast on chocolate truffles.

◆ TWELFTH NIGHT CAKE ◆

INGREDIENTS

250g (8oz) unsalted butter, softened, plus extra for greasing
250g (8oz) soft dark brown sugar
150ml (¼ pint) port
150ml (¼ pint) brandy
750g (1½lb) mixed dried fruit
125g (4oz) dried apricots, chopped
60g (2oz) mixed chopped peel
125g (4oz) glacé cherries, halved
1 tbsp grated orange zest
1 tbsp freshly squeezed orange juice
4 eggs (size 3)
250g (8oz) self-raising flour
1 tbsp ground mixed spice
90g (3oz) flaked almonds

DECORATION

3 tbsp apricot jam, boiled and sieved
900g (1¾lb) white marzipan
icing sugar, for dusting
2 quantities royal icing (see opposite)
red and green food colouring
2m (2yd) red or green ribbons

ILLUSTRATED ON PAGE 179

TWELFTH NIGHT CAKE USED TO BE SPECIALLY MADE TO MARK THE FEAST OF EPIPHANY. IT WAS ALWAYS A RICH FRUIT CAKE COVERED WITH ALMONDS OR ALMOND PASTE, BUT BY THE 19TH CENTURY THE CAKE HAD BECOME A MASTERPIECE OF DECORATION, WITH PIPING AND GILDING FAR BEYOND MOST COOKS' CAPABILITIES. TODAY, IT IS SIMPLY A CHRISTMAS CAKE, COVERED WITH MARZIPAN AND ICING.

MAKES A 23CM (9IN) CAKE

1 Place the butter, sugar, port and brandy in a large pan and bring to the boil. Stir in the mixed fruit, apricots, mixed peel and cherries until well blended. Return to the boil and simmer very gently for 15 minutes. Leave the mixture to cool overnight.

2 Lightly grease a 23cm (9in) round cake tin. Line the base and sides with a double thickness of non-stick baking parchment. Secure a double thickness strip of brown paper around the outside of the tin, then stand the tin on a baking sheet lined with 3–4 layers of brown paper. Preheat the oven to 160°C/300°F/gas 2.

3 Beat the orange zest and juice with the eggs. Sift the flour and spice into a large bowl and stir in the almonds. Add the beaten eggs and the dried mixed fruit to the flour, stir until well mixed then beat for 1 minute.

4 Place the mixture in the prepared tin, smooth the top and bake in the oven for 3–3¼ hours, or until a skewer inserted into the centre of the cake comes out clean. Leave to cool in the tin.

5 Turn out the cake, leaving the lining paper in place. Wrap the cake securely in foil and store in a cool place for up to 3–4 months until ready to decorate.

DECORATING THE CAKE

1 Place the cake in the centre of a cake board and brush with the apricot jam. Knead three-quarters of the marzipan into a round, reserving the remainder. Roll out the marzipan on a surface lightly dusted with icing sugar to form a round 7cm (3in) larger than the top of the cake.

2 Place the marzipan over the cake and smooth the top and sides with your hands. Trim off the marzipan at the base of the cake. Leave in a warm place to dry overnight.

3 Knead the trimmings and reserved marzipan together. Colour a tiny piece red. Cut the remainder in half and colour one piece light green and the other dark green. Roll out the dark green marzipan thinly and cut out holly leaves, using a small cutter. Roll out the light green marzipan and cut out ivy leaves, using a small cutter. Mould tiny berries with the red marzipan.

4 Make the royal icing (see opposite). Using a palette knife, spread the top of the cake with a thin, even layer of icing. Hold an icing ruler or long palette knife at a slight angle and draw it across the cake towards you in a continuous movement to make a smooth surface. Leave for 3–4 hours to dry.

5 Repeat to give a second layer of icing and leave to dry. Spread the remaining icing smoothly over the side of the cake. Using a small palette knife, press into the surface of the icing on the side and pull away gently to form peaks. Leave to dry overnight.

6 Arrange the holly leaves and berries on top of the cake and secure with a little icing. Fit the ribbon around the cake and the cake board and secure with a little icing or pins. Leave in a cake tin in a warm dry place to set overnight. If uncut, the cake will keep in a tin for up to 1 year.

PANETTONE

INGREDIENTS

450g (14oz) plain strong white flour,
plus extra for dusting
1 tsp salt
45g (1½oz) caster sugar
2 sachets easy-blend dried yeast
125g (4oz) unsalted butter, melted
150ml (¼ pint) milk
1 tsp vanilla essence
1 egg (size 3), plus 2 yolks
vegetable oil, for brushing
knob of butter, plus extra for greasing
125g (4oz) glacé fruits
90g (3oz) sultanas
2 tsp grated lemon zest
icing sugar, for dusting

THIS LIGHT, AIRY CAKE IS THE ITALIAN VERSION OF CHRISTMAS CAKE.

SERVES 6–8

1 Sift the flour, salt, sugar and yeast into a warm mixing bowl, or food processor fitted with a dough beater.

2 Add the melted butter to the milk, then beat in the vanilla, egg and egg yolks. Mix into the flour to form a soft dough. Knead for 8–10 minutes, or 2–3 minutes in a food processor, until smooth and elastic. Brush with oil, cover with clingfilm and leave in a warm place for 1–2 hours, until doubled in size.

3 Meanwhile, lightly grease a 15cm (6in) round cake tin and line the base with non-stick baking parchment. Dust the inside with flour. Stand the tin on a baking sheet and tie a piece of foil around the outside of the tin to stand 7cm (3in) above the rim.

4 Knead the dough for 1–2 minutes until smooth, then roll out into a flat round. Mix together the glacé fruits, sultanas and lemon zest, scatter over the surface of the dough and press in with the rolling pin.

5 Knead the dough until smooth. Gather into a ball and cut a cross in the top with scissors. Place in the cake tin, cover carefully with oiled clingfilm and leave in a warm place to rise until the centre touches the clingfilm. Preheat the oven to 200°C/400°F/gas 6.

6 Remove the clingfilm, re-cut the cross and place a knob of butter in the centre. Bake for 10 minutes, then lower the heat to 180°C/350°F/gas 4 and bake for 40–45 minutes, until a skewer inserted into the centre comes out clean. Cool in the tin for 10 minutes, remove the foil and ease the cake out of the tin. Cool on a wire rack. Dust with icing sugar before serving.

WREATH CAKE

INGREDIENTS

90g (3oz) almonds, chopped
90g (3oz) sultanas
90g (3oz) raisins
90g (3oz) glacé cherries, halved
60g (2oz) mixed chopped peel
2 tbsp sherry
175g (6oz) self-raising wholemeal flour
1 tsp ground cardamom
175g (6oz) moist light brown sugar
175g (6oz) unsalted butter, softened, plus extra
for greasing
3 eggs (size 3)

DECORATION

3 tbsp apricot jam, boiled and sieved
750g (1½lb) white marzipan
dark green food colouring
icing sugar, for dusting
marzipan fruit and leaves (see page 178)
2 tbsp royal icing (see below)

ILLUSTRATED ON PAGE *179*

THIS SCANDINAVIAN CAKE MAKES A STUNNING CENTREPIECE FOR THE CHRISTMAS TABLE.

SERVES 10

1 Preheat the oven to 160C°/300°F/gas 2. Grease a 23cm (9in) ring mould and place a circle of non-stick baking parchment at the bottom.

2 Mix together the almonds, sultanas, raisins, cherries, mixed peel and sherry.

3 Sift the flour and cardamom into a bowl and add the sugar, butter and eggs. Mix well, then beat for 2–3 minutes until smooth and glossy. Fold the fruit and nuts into the mixture until evenly distributed.

4 Place the mixture in the tin, smooth the surface and cook in the oven for 1 hour–1 hour 10 minutes until the cake feels firm to the touch. Test by inserting a skewer into the centre of the cake – it should come out clean. Allow the cake to cool in the tin, then invert on to a wire rack and remove the paper.

5 Brush the cake evenly with the apricot glaze. Colour the marzipan leaf green and knead until evenly coloured. Roll out on a surface dusted with icing sugar to form a round 5cm (2in) larger than the cake. Cut a small circle out of the centre, then place the marzipan over the centre of the ring.

6 Ease the marzipan around the inside of the cake and smooth over the top and down the sides, trimming off the excess at the base. Place the cake on a cake board or plate, store in a box or tin with a lid and leave in a warm dry place to set overnight.

7 Arrange the marzipan fruit and leaves evenly over the cake, bending the leaves to shape. Use a little royal icing to make them stick firmly.

ROYAL ICING

INGREDIENTS

2 egg whites (size 3)
¼ tsp lemon juice
500g (1lb) icing sugar, sieved
1 tsp glycerine

MAKES ENOUGH TO COVER A 15CM (6IN) CAKE

1 Stir the egg whites and lemon juice in a bowl. Mix in enough icing sugar to give the consistency of unwhipped cream.

2 Add the remaining icing sugar a little at a time, gently beating after each addition, until the icing is smooth and white and stands in soft peaks.

3 Stir in the glycerine until the icing is well blended. Place in an airtight container, or cover the bowl with a damp tea towel until ready to use. Scrape down the sides of the bowl while icing to prevent it drying out.

POLISH SPICED CAKE

INGREDIENTS
1 tbsp melted butter
1 tbsp fresh white breadcrumbs
250g (8oz) butter
250g (8oz) caster sugar
60ml (2fl oz) water
3 eggs (size 3), separated
250g (8oz) self-raising flour
1½ tsp ground mixed spice
30g (1oz) chopped angelica
30g (1oz) mixed chopped peel
60g (2oz) glacé cherries, chopped
60g (2oz) walnuts, chopped
icing sugar, for dusting
fresh holly, to decorate

THE MOST IMPORTANT HOLIDAY OF THE YEAR IN POLAND IS NEW YEAR'S EVE. SPICED CAKE IS ALWAYS SERVED, PREFERABLY WITH VODKA.

SERVES 6–8

1 Preheat the oven to 180°C/350°F/gas 4. Brush a 20cm (8in), 1.5 litre (2½ pint) fluted ring mould with melted butter and coat with breadcrumbs.

2 Place the butter, sugar and water in a pan and heat gently, stirring occasionally, until melted. Bring to the boil, boil for 3 minutes until syrupy, then allow to cool.

3 Place the egg whites in a clean bowl and whisk until they stand in stiff peaks.

4 Sift the flour and mixed spice into a bowl, add the angelica, mixed peel, cherries and walnuts and mix well. Stir in the egg yolks.

5 Pour the cooled syrup into the flour mixture and beat with a wooden spoon to form a soft batter. Using a plastic spatula, gradually fold in the egg whites until the mixture is evenly blended.

6 Pour the mixture into the prepared mould and lightly smooth the surface. Bake in the preheated oven for 50–60 minutes, or until the cake springs back when pressed in the centre. Turn out and cool on a wire rack. To serve, dust thickly with icing sugar and decorate with a sprig of holly.

NORWEGIAN MACAROON CAKE

INGREDIENTS
500g (1lb) ground almonds
15g (½oz) plain flour
500g (1lb) caster sugar
1 tbsp finely grated lemon zest
1 tsp almond essence
3 egg whites (size 3), whisked
ICING
1 tsp orange-flower water
1 egg white (size 3)
250g (8oz) icing sugar, sieved
DECORATION
fresh fruit and bay leaves
icing sugar, for dusting

ILLUSTRATED BELOW
THIS CAKE IS A FAVOURITE FOR BIRTHDAY, WEDDING AND CHRISTMAS CELEBRATIONS. THE TOWERING CONFECTION CAN BE UP TO 60CM (2FT) TALL, ADORNED WITH ICING, FLOWERS, GLACE FRUITS AND NUTS.

SERVES 20

1 Preheat the oven to 160°C/ 325°F/ gas 3. Line 3–4 baking sheets with non-stick baking parchment.

2 Mix together the ground almonds, flour, caster sugar, lemon zest and almond essence in a bowl until evenly blended.

3 Gradually stir in enough egg white to form a soft but firm dough. Divide into manageable pieces and roll out each piece into a rope as thick as a finger.

4 To construct the cake, the "ropes" are cut into 12 graduated lengths, and formed into circles. Start by cutting a piece 10cm (4in) long. Form into a circle, pressing the ends together to join neatly, and place on a baking sheet.

5 Continue to cut lengths and make circles, increasing the length by 2.5cm (1in) each time, until there are 12 graduated circles in total, the largest measuring 37.5cm (15in) in circumference.

6 Bake the circles in batches for 20 minutes until pale brown and firm. Leave to cool for 10 minutes, then slide on to a wire rack.

7 To make the icing, whisk the orange-flower water and egg white in a bowl. Gradually add the icing sugar, beating well after each addition, until it is the consistency of thick cream. Continue to beat and add the icing sugar until it stands in soft peaks.

8 Spoon the icing into a greaseproof paper piping bag fitted with a No. 1 plain writing nozzle. Alternatively, snip the point off the end of the bag, half-fill with icing and fold down the top.

9 Using a flat cake plate or a cake board, place the largest circle in the centre. Spread with a little icing and place the next largest circle on top. Repeat until all the circles are stacked together. Pipe fine threads of icing in loops around each ring until evenly covered. Decorate the base and top with fresh fruit and bay leaves and dust with icing sugar.

❖ PAVLOVA ❖

INGREDIENTS

5 egg whites (size 3)
290g (9½oz) caster sugar, plus extra for frosting
½ tsp vanilla essence
1½ tsp vinegar
1½ tsp cornflour
90g (3oz) white seedless grapes
90g (3oz) red seedless grapes
8 physalis, optional
90g (3oz) cherries
90g (3oz) strawberries
300ml (½ pint) double cream
150ml (¼ pint) Greek yogurt
125g (4oz) mixed glacé fruits, chopped

ILLUSTRATED ON PAGE *178*
THE LIGHT CRISP MERINGUE WITH A
MARSHMALLOW CENTRE WAS NAMED IN
HONOUR OF THE RUSSIAN PRIMA BALLERINA,
ANNA PAVLOVA. THIS FESTIVE VERSION IS
DECORATED WITH FROSTED FRUIT.

SERVES 6

1 Preheat the oven to 140°C/275°F/gas 1.
Line a baking sheet with non-stick baking
parchment and draw a 23cm (9in) circle in
the centre. Turn the paper over.

2 Place four egg whites in a clean bowl. Beat
by hand or with an electric whisk until the
whites are stiff. Gradually add the sugar,
whisking well after each addition until the
meringue is thick.

3 Blend together the vanilla essence, vinegar
and cornflour in a bowl and add to the
meringue. Whisk until the meringue is thick
and glossy and stands up in soft peaks.

4 Spoon the meringue into a large nylon
piping bag fitted with a large star nozzle.
Pipe a ring of shells following the marked
line. Fill in the centre with a coil of meringue.

5 Pipe another ring of shells on top of
the first ring and fill in the centre with the
remaining meringue. Alternatively, spread
the remaining meringue inside the circle and
smooth the top.

6 Bake in the oven for 1 hour, then turn off
the heat and leave the pavlova for 2–3
hours to become cold, without opening the
oven door. Store in an airtight container for
up to 2 weeks or until required.

7 Whisk the remaining egg white in a bowl.
Place some caster sugar in a bowl and line
a wire rack with kitchen paper.

8 Cut the white and red grapes into small
bunches, brush all over with egg white,
then dip into the caster sugar until coated
evenly. Place on the paper-covered rack and
leave in a warm place to dry. Frost the
physalis, if using, the cherries and the
strawberries in the same way.

9 Whip the cream and yogurt in a bowl
until just thickened. Add the glacé fruit
and fold in gently. Spoon the fruit and cream
into the centre of the pavlova and decorate
with the frosted fruit.

❖ MINCE PIES ❖

INGREDIENTS

375g (12oz) plain flour, plus extra for dusting
175g (6oz) butter
30g (1oz) caster sugar
1 egg yolk (size 3)
375g (12oz) mincemeat
icing sugar, to dust

THIS RECIPE DATES BACK TO MEDIEVAL TIMES.
MINCEMEAT WAS ORIGINALLY A MIXTURE
OF SHREDDED OR MINCED MEAT, DRIED FRUIT
AND SPICES – HENCE THE NAME – AND THE
MINCE PIE WAS LIKE A MODERN MEAT PIE.
SINCE THEN THE RECIPE HAS BECOME
SWEETER, AND THE MEAT HAS DISAPPEARED.

MAKES 20

1 Preheat the oven to 200°C/400°F/gas 6. Sift
the flour into a bowl, add the butter and
rub in lightly with the fingers until the
mixture resembles breadcrumbs.

2 Using a fork, stir in the sugar, egg yolk and
enough cold water to mix to a soft dough.
Knead gently on a lightly floured surface.

3 Roll out the pastry thinly and cut out 20 x
7cm (3in) rounds and 20 x 5cm (2in)
rounds, using fluted cutters. Knead the
trimmings together and re-roll as necessary.

4 Dust 20 x 7cm (3in) tartlet tins with flour
and line with the larger pastry circles.
Prick the base of each one with a fork and
half-fill with mincemeat. Brush the edges of
each smaller circle with water, invert, and
press on top of each tart to seal the edges.

5 With the point of a knife, pierce a hole in
the centre of each tart lid to allow the
steam to escape. Bake in the preheated oven
for 15–20 minutes until light brown. Cool on
a wire rack before removing from the tins,
and dust with icing sugar before serving.

FESTIVE CAKES & BISCUITS

THIS ENTICING COLLECTION OFFERS SOMETHING FOR EVERYONE, from a traditional English fruit cake, covered with royal icing, to the entrancing Scandinavian wreath cake, decorated with an intricate, interwoven pattern of marzipan fruit and leaves. An elegant pavlova, filled with frosted fruit and cream, strikes a lighter note. Other traditional offerings include rich chocolate truffles, shortbread, spiced biscuits to hang on the tree, gingerbread men and pig fairings, tied with ribbons.

Twelfth Night Cake
p.174 & top right
Pavlova p.177 & centre left
Wreath Cake p.175 & centre

Pig Fairings p.183 & far left
St Nicholas Spice Biscuits
p.182 & far left
Chocolate Truffles p.183 & top
Hogmanay Shortbread
p.183 & bottom right

Stollen

ILLUSTRATED ON PAGE 167

INGREDIENTS

60g (2oz) raisins
60g (2oz) currants
60g (2oz) candied citrus peel, chopped
60g (2oz) glacé cherries, halved
30g (1oz) angelica, chopped
3 tbsp dark rum
375g (12oz) plain strong white flour,
plus extra for flouring
¼ tsp salt
2 sachets easy-blend dried yeast
90g (3oz) caster sugar
1 tsp grated lemon zest
¼ tsp almond essence
125ml (4fl oz) milk, warmed
2 eggs (size 3)
125g (4oz) unsalted butter, softened
30g (1oz) flaked almonds
icing sugar, for dusting

THIS GERMAN FRUIT BREAD WILL KEEP FOR UP TO 1 MONTH, AND THE FLAVOUR IMPROVES WITH KEEPING.

SERVES 12

1 Mix the raisins, currants, peel, cherries, angelica and rum in a bowl. Cover and leave for several hours, or overnight. Drain thoroughly, reserving the rum.

2 Sift the flour and salt into a warm bowl. Stir in the dried yeast, half the sugar and the lemon zest.

3 Place the almond essence, warm milk, eggs and reserved rum in a separate bowl. Whisk until blended evenly. Add this liquid to the flour with 90g (3oz) of the butter, cut into small pieces. Mix together with a wooden spoon and beat until smooth.

4 Turn the dough out on to a lightly floured surface and knead for about 10 minutes until smooth and elastic. Alternatively, use a mixer or food processor. Melt the remaining butter. Place the dough in a clean bowl. Brush the bowl and dough with the butter, cover with clingfilm and leave for 30 minutes.

5 Knead the dough until smooth, return to the bowl and cover. Place in a warm place until doubled in size, about 1-2 hours.

6 Turn out the dough, punch it down to remove air bubbles and knead into a round. Flatten out the dough to a thickness of 1cm (½in). Sprinkle the soaked fruit and the almonds over the surface, then press into the dough. Gather up and knead lightly to distribute the fruit. Roll out to form an oblong measuring 30 x 20cm (12 x 8in).

7 Brush with butter and sprinkle with the remaining sugar. Fold one end into the middle and press down. Bring the opposite side over the fold. Using floured hands, press down the ends and taper them slightly.

8 Line a swiss roll tin with non-stick baking parchment. Place the loaf on the tin and brush with melted butter. Cover loosely with a tea towel and leave until doubled in size, about 30 minutes. Preheat the oven to 190°C/ 375°F/gas 5.

9 Bake in the oven for 30–40 minutes until golden brown. Cool on a wire rack and dust with icing sugar to serve. To keep, wrap securely in foil or clingfilm.

Greek Honey Cake

INGREDIENTS

275g (9oz) clear honey
½ tsp ground cloves
½ tsp ground cinnamon
½ tsp ground nutmeg
90g (3oz) butter, softened
90g (3oz) soft dark brown sugar
3 eggs (size 3), separated
1 tsp bicarbonate of soda
250g (8oz) plain flour
1 tsp baking powder
90g (3oz) mixed dried fruit
90g (3oz) walnuts, chopped
warm honey and walnut halves, to decorate

SPICED HONEY CAKE IS BEST MADE 2 MONTHS BEFORE CHRISTMAS TO ALLOW THE FLAVOURS TO DEVELOP, AND TO ALLOW THE CAKE TO ABSORB THE SYRUP.

MAKES ONE 20CM (8IN) SQUARE CAKE

1 Line the base and sides of an 18cm (7in) deep square cake tin with non-stick baking parchment. Preheat the oven to 160°C/325°F/gas 3.

2 Heat the honey, cloves, cinnamon and nutmeg in a pan, bring to the boil, then allow to cool.

3 Place the butter and sugar in a bowl and beat with a wooden spoon until light and fluffy. Add the egg yolks one at a time, beating well after each addition.

4 Add the honey mixture and bicarbonate of soda and beat until smooth.

5 Sift in the flour and baking powder. Fold in gently using a spatula until all the flour has been incorporated.

6 Whisk the egg whites in a clean bowl until stiff. Fold gently into the mixture with the fruit and nuts until evenly blended, then pour into the prepared tin and smooth the top with a spatula or knife.

7 Bake in the oven for 1 hour–1 hour 10 minutes until the cake is well risen and golden brown, and the top springs back when pressed in the centre.

8 Leave the cake to cool in the tin, then turn out on to a wire rack and remove the lining paper. Wrap the cake in clingfilm or foil and store for 1–2 days before eating as the flavour and texture improve with keeping. To serve, glaze the top with warm honey and decorate with halved walnuts.

Fougasse Christmas Bread

INGREDIENTS

500g (1lb) plain strong white flour,
plus extra for flouring
¼ tsp salt
2 sachets easy-blend dried yeast
60g (2oz) light soft brown sugar
grated zest and juice of 1 orange
150ml (¼ pint) olive oil, plus extra for oiling
2 eggs (size 3)
an assortment of fresh and dried fruit, nuts
and sweetmeats, such as apples, pears, figs,
grapes, pomegranates, dried dates, dried
figs, raisins, walnuts, almonds, chestnuts,
hazelnuts and nougat

ILLUSTRATED ON PAGE 153
THIS ENRICHED BREAD FORMS THE
CENTREPIECE OF THE "THIRTEEN DESSERTS"
OF PROVENCE AND SYMBOLIZES CHRIST.
THE TWELVE APOSTLES ARE REPRESENTED
BY LOCAL PRODUCE SUCH AS NUTS,
SWEETMEATS, FRESH AND DRIED FRUIT.
THE DISPLAY IS LEFT ON THE TABLE AND
REPLENISHED AS NECESSARY UNTIL
TWELFTH NIGHT.

SERVES 12

1 Sift the flour and salt into a bowl, add the yeast, sugar and orange zest and mix together until evenly blended.

2 Measure the orange juice and make up to 300ml (½ pint) with hot water. Pour into a bowl and beat with the oil and eggs. Add to the flour mixture and mix together with a wooden spoon to form a soft dough.

3 Turn out on to a lightly floured surface and knead for 10 minutes until smooth and no longer sticky. Alternatively, use a food mixer or processor.

4 Place the dough in a clean, oiled bowl, cover with clingfilm, and set in a warm place for at least 1 hour until doubled in size.

5 Turn the dough out on to the floured surface and knead for 1–2 minutes until smooth and elastic. Cut in half and roll out one piece into a 20cm (8in) round. Keep the remaining half covered.

6 Preheat the oven to 220°C/425°F/gas 7. Transfer the dough round to an oiled baking sheet. Using a sharp knife, make 12 deep cuts, radiating out from the centre. With lightly oiled hands pull the dough gently to open up the cuts. Cover with oiled clingfilm and leave to rise for 20–30 minutes. Repeat to shape the remaining dough.

7 Bake the bread for 20–25 minutes until well risen and golden brown, covering loosely with foil to prevent over-browning. Cool on a wire rack.

8 Place the bread on a tray or large platter surrounded by the 12 items representing the Apostles: fresh and dried fruit, raisins, sultanas, nuts and nougat.

Gingerbread House

INGREDIENTS

6 tbsp (90ml) golden syrup
2 tbsp black treacle
90g (3oz) light soft brown sugar
90g (3oz) butter
500g (1lb) plain flour, plus extra for flouring
1 tbsp ground ginger
1 tbsp bicarbonate of soda
2 egg yolks
DECORATION
1 quantity royal icing (see page 175)
assorted coloured sweets
icing sugar, for dusting

MANY GERMAN CUSTOMS ASSOCIATED WITH
CHRISTMAS DATE BACK TO THE MIDDLE AGES.
THE SPICED BISCUITS AND CAKES ALWAYS
MADE AT THIS TIME ARE OFTEN ASSOCIATED
WITH SPECIFIC CITIES: GINGERBREAD
COMES FROM NUREMBERG.

SERVES 20

1 Cut out the templates for the house, using the guides on page 189. Preheat the oven to 190°C/ 375°F/gas 5. Line 3–4 baking sheets with non-stick baking parchment. Place the syrup, treacle, sugar and butter in a pan and heat gently, stirring occasionally, until melted.

2 Sift the flour, ginger and bicarbonate of soda into a bowl. Add the egg yolks and stir in the syrup mixture with a wooden spoon to form a soft dough. Knead on a lightly floured surface until smooth.

3 Cut off one-third of the dough and wrap the remainder in clingfilm. Roll out the one-third of dough thinly on a baking sheet. Place the template for the side walls at one end and cut out neatly with a sharp knife. Repeat to cut another wall shape. Remove the trimmings, knead together and re-roll on another baking sheet.

4 Bake the cut-out wall shapes in the oven for 8-10 minutes until the gingerbread is golden brown. Cool on the baking sheet. Repeat with the remaining dough to make the other walls, and the roof.

5 Make the royal icing following the recipe on page 175. Spoon some of the icing into a greaseproof paper piping bag fitted with a No. 2 plain writing nozzle. Pipe lines, loops and dots around the windows, doors, walls and roof to decorate and leave flat to dry.

6 To assemble the house, pipe a line of icing on the side edges of the main walls and side walls. Stick them together on a 25cm (10in) cake board to form a box shape.

7 Pipe a line of icing following the pitch of the roof on both end pieces and along the top of the two roof pieces. Press gently into position. Use books or small boxes to support the underneath of each overhanging roof piece while the icing sets, about 15–20 minutes (see page 189).

8 Pipe the finishing touches to the roof and base of the house. Use icing to stick the coloured sweets in position along the seams and around the base of the house. Dust the cake board and house with icing sugar.

New Year's Eve Fritters

INGREDIENTS
300g (10oz) plain strong white flour
¼ tsp salt
30g (1oz) caster sugar
1 sachet easy-blend dried yeast
200ml (7fl oz) milk, warmed
2 eggs (size 3)
FILLING
60g (2oz) currants
60g (2oz) raisins
30g (1oz) crystallized orange peel, chopped
1 tbsp freshly grated lemon zest
vegetable oil, for deep frying
icing sugar, for dusting

THESE DELICIOUS FRITTERS FROM HOLLAND ARE MADE WITH A YEAST DOUGH PACKED WITH FRUIT, CANDIED PEEL AND LEMON ZEST. DROPPED INTO HOT OIL, THEY PUFF UP TO FORM CRISP, GOLDEN FRUIT DOUGHNUTS.

MAKES 20

1 Sift the flour and salt into a warm bowl, and stir in the sugar and yeast.

2 Add the milk and eggs and mix together with a wooden spoon to form a soft dough. Beat the dough until it is smooth and just holds its shape on the spoon.

3 Cover the bowl with clingfilm and leave in a warm place for about 1 hour until the dough has doubled in size.

4 Mix together the currants, raisins, peel and lemon zest in a bowl. Add to the dough and stir until evenly distributed. Cover with clingfilm.

5 Pour oil into a deep-fryer to a depth of about 10cm (4in). Heat the oil to 170°C/340°F, or until a cube of bread dropped into the oil browns in 30 seconds.

6 Using a tablespoon, scoop out one spoonful of dough and carefully drop into the oil. Fry 4 fritters at a time, turning them with a slotted spoon until golden brown. Drain on a wire rack covered with kitchen paper and repeat with the remaining dough.

7 Dust the fritters with icing sugar and serve warm or cold.

St Nicholas Spice Biscuits

INGREDIENTS
250g (8oz) self-raising flour
¼ tsp of each ground spice: cinnamon, nutmeg, anise, mace, cloves, cardamom and ginger
125g (4oz) light brown sugar
60g (2oz) ground almonds
125g (4oz) unsalted butter, softened
1 egg (size 3), beaten
60g (2oz) flaked almonds
30g (1oz) currants
DECORATION
1 quantity royal icing (see page 175)
red, yellow and green food colouring
2mm (⅛in) wide coloured ribbons

ILLUSTRATED ON PAGE 178
IN HOLLAND THESE BISCUITS ARE TRADITIONALLY SHAPED IN WOODEN MOULDS.

MAKES 24

1 Preheat the oven to 190°C/375°F/gas 5. Line 3–4 baking sheets with non-stick baking parchment.

2 Sift the flour and spices into a bowl. Stir in the sugar, ground almonds and the butter, cut into small pieces. Rub in with the fingers until the mixture resembles fine breadcrumbs. Stir in just enough egg to bind the mixture together. Knead into a neat ball.

3 Roll out the dough thinly, and cut out shapes using a gingerbread man cutter, or other cutters. Place the biscuits on the baking sheets and decorate the gingerbread men with flaked almonds, or currants. To make hanging decorations, use a drinking straw to form a hole at the top of each shape. Bake for 10–15 minutes until golden brown. Cool on the tray, then transfer to a wire rack.

4 Divide the royal icing into 3 portions and colour them red, yellow and green. Spoon each colour into a greaseproof paper icing bag, fold down the top and snip off the point.

5 Outline some of the shapes with a line of icing, and fill in the shapes with lines and dots, varying the colours. Leave in a cool place to dry. Use coloured ribbons to hang some of the biscuits on the Christmas tree.

Marzipan Fruit

INGREDIENTS
250g (8oz) white marzipan
green, yellow and orange food colouring
whole cloves, cut in half

DECORATE CAKES, OR THE CHRISTMAS TABLE, WITH THIS ASSORTMENT OF FRUIT.

MAKES 40

1 Divide the marzipan into 4 pieces. Colour 2 pieces light and dark green; colour the remainder yellow and orange.

2 Using pea-sized pieces, mould the light green, orange and yellow marzipan into apple, pear and orange shapes. Texture the oranges by rubbing gently on a fine grater. Insert a clove top into each fruit as a stalk, and the end as a calyx.

3 Using the dark green marzipan and a small leaf cutter, cut out holly, ivy and vine leaves. Mark the veins by pressing a real leaf on to the marzipan leaf, then bend the leaves to shape.

4 Leave to dry in a warm place overnight. To decorate a cake, use a little icing to hold the shapes in position.

ᐳ PIG FAIRINGS ᐸ

INGREDIENTS

175g (6oz) self-raising flour,
plus extra for flouring
1 tsp ground ginger
1 tsp nutmeg
finely grated zest of 1 lemon
125g (4oz) clotted cream, or unsalted butter
90g (3oz) soft brown sugar
60g (2oz) currants
1 egg (size 3), beaten
2mm (⅛in) wide coloured ribbon, to decorate

ILLUSTRATED ON PAGE 178
THESE CORNISH GINGER BISCUITS ARE
BAKED IN MANY SHAPES – STARS, HEARTS AND
GINGERBREAD MEN, AS WELL AS PIGS – TO
DISPLAY IN SHOPS AND MARKETS DURING
ADVENT, TIED WITH FESTIVE RIBBON.

MAKES 60

1 Sift the flour and spices into a bowl. Stir in the lemon zest, clotted cream and sugar and mix with a fork. If using butter, rub in finely with the fingers.

2 Add 45g (1½oz) of the currants and the egg and mix to form a firm dough. Knead on a lightly floured surface until smooth, wrap in clingfilm and chill for 1 hour.

3 Line 2 baking trays with non-stick baking parchment and preheat the oven to 190°C/375°F/gas 5.

4 Roll out the dough on a lightly floured surface until 6mm (¼in) thick. Using a pig-shaped cutter, or other biscuit cutter, cut out about 60 shapes, kneading and re-rolling the trimmings when necessary.

5 Arrange the shapes well apart on the baking sheets, press a currant in position for each eye, and bake in the oven for 10–15 minutes. Leave on the sheet to cool for 10 minutes, then transfer to a wire rack.

6 Tie each biscuit "pig" around the neck with coloured ribbon, and arrange on a serving plate, or tie on to the Christmas tree.

ᐳ HOGMANAY SHORTBREAD ᐸ

INGREDIENTS

175g (6oz) plain flour,
plus extra for flouring
60g (2oz) caster sugar,
plus extra for sprinkling
60g (2oz) cornflour or ground rice
125g (4oz) unsalted butter, diced

ILLUSTRATED ON PAGE 179
SCOTTISH SHORTBREAD IS TRADITIONALLY
SHAPED IN WOODEN MOULDS AND CUT INTO
TRIANGLES CALLED "PETTICOAT TAILS".

MAKES 12

1 Preheat the oven to 160°C/325°F/gas 3. Mix together 1 teaspoon each of plain flour and caster sugar and use to dust a 10cm (4in) shortbread mould, if available. If not, use 10cm (4in) biscuit cutters. Line a baking sheet with non-stick baking parchment.

2 Sift the flour, cornflour and sugar into a mixing bowl. Rub in the butter finely with your fingers until the mixture begins to bind together. Knead into a firm dough.

3 Cut the dough into 12 pieces. Roll out one piece on a lightly floured surface to the size of the mould, if using. Place the dough in the mould and press to fit neatly. Using a palette knife, trim off the excess dough. Invert on to the baking sheet and tap firmly to release the shape. Repeat with the remaining dough, re-flouring the mould each time.

4 If not using a mould, roll out the dough on a floured surface to a thickness of 6mm (¼in) and cut out 12 shapes with biscuit cutters. Bake in the oven for 35–40 minutes until pale in colour.

5 Sprinkle the top of the shortbread with a little caster sugar and leave to cool on the baking sheet.

ᐳ CHOCOLATE TRUFFLES ᐸ

INGREDIENTS

125ml (4fl oz) double cream
2 tbsp dark rum, brandy or sherry
250g (8oz) plain, white or milk chocolate, melted
COATINGS
2 tsp cocoa
1 tsp icing sugar
60g (2oz) white or plain chocolate, grated
2 tbsp chocolate vermicelli
60g (2oz) plain chocolate, melted
60g (2oz) finely chopped nuts

ILLUSTRATED ON PAGE 179
CHOCOLATE TRUFFLES ARE ALWAYS A
FAVOURITE AT CHRISTMAS TIME. PACK THEM
INTO PRETTY BOXES AS A GIFT, OR PILE THEM
HIGH ON A DECORATIVE PLATE.

MAKES 30

1 Place the cream in a pan, bring to the boil to sterilize, then cool until warm. Stir in the rum, brandy or sherry when the mixture is lukewarm, then add it to the cool, melted chocolate, stirring until evenly blended.

2 Beat the mixture until light and fluffy, then chill for 2–3 hours until it is firm enough to divide into portions.

3 Using a teaspoon, scoop out balls of the mixture on to a tray lined with kitchen paper, keeping them well apart. Chill until firm, about 1 hour, then roll each portion of truffle mixture into a neat ball.

4 Sieve the cocoa and icing sugar together on to a plate and roll some of the truffles in the mixture to coat evenly. Repeat, coating the remaining truffles in grated chocolate, chocolate vermicelli, melted chocolate or nuts. Chill until set.

COUNTDOWN TO CHRISTMAS

TEN WEEKS AHEAD

❧ *Read Christmas editions of magazines for ideas*
❧ *Visit Christmas departments to see what is available*
❧ *Write out a gift list and decide what to make and what to buy*
❧ *Design and plan a gift-filled advent calendar (see page 120)*
❧ *Design Christmas cards and gift wrap*
❧ *Gather odds and ends that will be useful for finishing touches,*
such as leaves, seed pods, buttons, ribbons, sequins, beads, shells and boxes

Shells
Collect seashells
on your summer
holiday, or buy
polished ones in
a shell shop

EIGHT WEEKS AHEAD

❧ *Buy materials for cards, gifts and advent calendar*
❧ *Make advent calendar (see page 120)*
❧ *Decide what type of tree to use (see pages 14–17)*
❧ *Start making Christmas cards and gifts*
❧ *Make Christmas stockings (see page 118)*
❧ *Plan theme for tree decorations and decide what to make and what to buy*
❧ *Make Greek Honey Cake (see page 180) and store wrapped in foil*

SIX WEEKS AHEAD

❧ *Begin gift shopping*
❧ *Start making tree decorations*
❧ *Check last posting dates and buy stamps*
❧ *Plan your Christmas menu*
❧ *Add a few extra special Christmas items to weekly shopping*
❧ *Make Twelfth Night Cake (see page 174), Wreath Cake (see page 175)*
and Christmas Pudding (see page 168) and wrap in foil

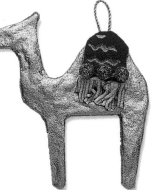

Salt Dough Camel
(see pages 20–21)
Make salt dough tree
decorations six weeks
before Christmas

FOUR WEEKS AHEAD

❧ *Print gift wrap (see pages 100–101)*
❧ *Make gift boxes to fit gifts (see page 102)*
❧ *Start using advent calendar and let children write to Santa*
❧ *Plan theme for dining table and make festive table decorations,*
such as crackers (see pages 142–43) and painted glassware (see pages 126–27)
❧ *Make decorations using dried and artificial ingredients, such as wreaths*
(see pages 50–55), door swags (see pages 56–57) and garlands (see pages 60–63)
❧ *Plan lighting, such as lanterns (see page 86–87) or a twig chandelier (see page 81)*
❧ *Order special food as necessary, such as turkey, goose or fish*

TWO WEEKS AHEAD

ᴥ *Get table linen laundered and decorate if desired (see pages 130–31)*
ᴥ *Buy a fresh tree and keep it in water in a cool place;*
bring it indoors as late as possible
ᴥ *Test tree lights and replace broken bulbs*
ᴥ *Stock up on candles*
ᴥ *Look for supplies of holly and evergreens*
ᴥ *Shop for non-perishable food*
ᴥ *Make dishes that can be frozen, such as stuffings (see pages 158–59),*
soups (see pages 148–49) and mince pies (see page 177)
ᴥ *Ice Twelfth Night Cake (see page 174)*
ᴥ *Make Panettone (see page 175) and store in foil*
ᴥ *Make Pavlova shell (see page 177) and store in an airtight container*

Embroidered napkins
(see page 131)
Use gold thread to
embroider a festive
motif on table napkins

ONE WEEK AHEAD

ᴥ *Decorate the tree*
ᴥ *Wrap and decorate gifts*
ᴥ *Make decorations using evergreens, such as*
a kissing bough (see pages 68–71)
ᴥ *Make gingerbread angels for the tree (see page 40–42)*
ᴥ *Decorate the house with shop-bought and home-made decorations*
ᴥ *Make Cranberry Sauce (see page 165)*
ᴥ *Make Truffles (see page 183) and refrigerate*
ᴥ *Make Cumberland Rum Butter (see page 168)*
ᴥ *Make Gingerbread House pieces (see page 181) and store in a cake box*
ᴥ *Make biscuits and shortbread (see pages 182–83) and store in an airtight container*

Gift boxes
(see page 102)
Start to wrap gifts one
week before Christmas

THREE OR FOUR DAYS AHEAD

ᴥ *Arrange flowers (see page 66–67)*
ᴥ *Make a fresh garland (see page 60–63)*
ᴥ *Shop for last-minute food items*
ᴥ *Make or buy lots of ice for festive drinks*
ᴥ *Boil ham and refrigerate (see page 156)*

CHRISTMAS EVE

ᴥ *Make a fruit and flower display (see page 72)*
ᴥ *Prepare as much of the festive meal as possible*
ᴥ *Defrost frozen food, allowing 24 hours for large turkeys or geese*
ᴥ *Lay the table if possible*
ᴥ *Put champagne on ice*
ᴥ *Hang stockings*

Fresh holly
Make fresh decorations as
close to the day as possible

TEMPLATES

Use the templates on the following pages for specific projects or simply to help design festive gift tags, cards, block prints and tree decorations. The grid will help you to enlarge or reduce the designs proportionally.

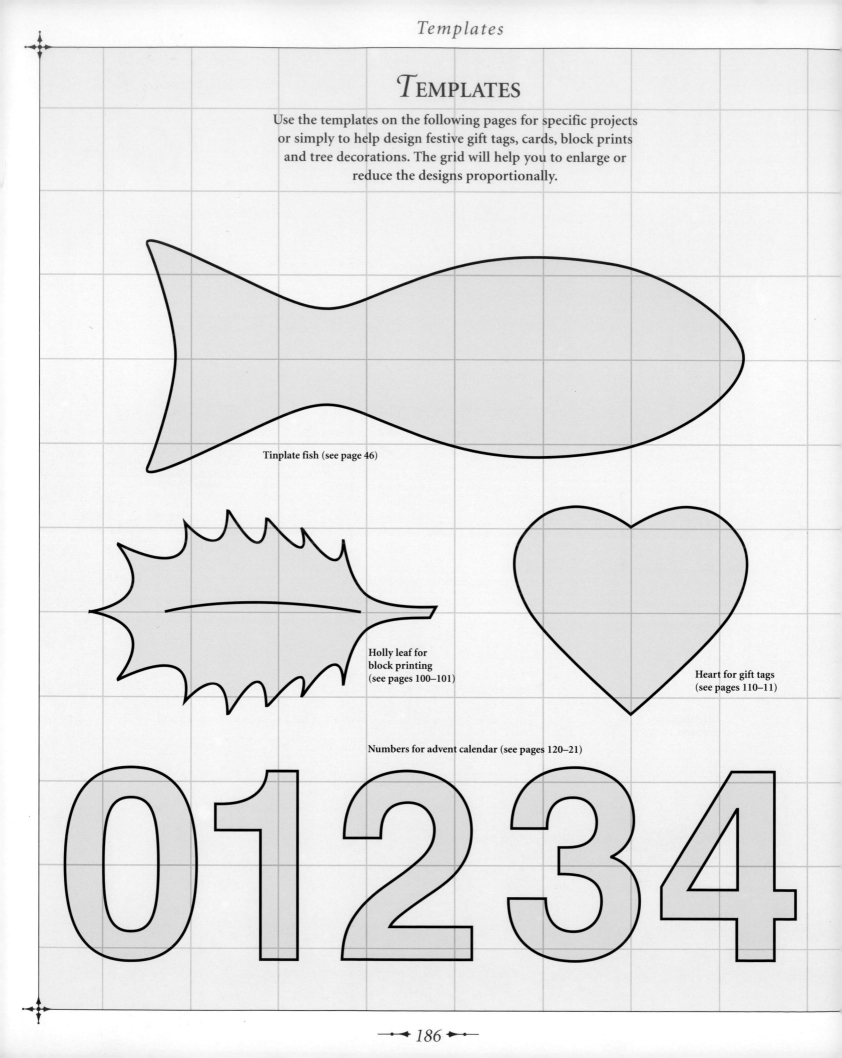

Tinplate fish (see page 46)

Holly leaf for block printing (see pages 100–101)

Heart for gift tags (see pages 110–11)

Numbers for advent calendar (see pages 120–21)

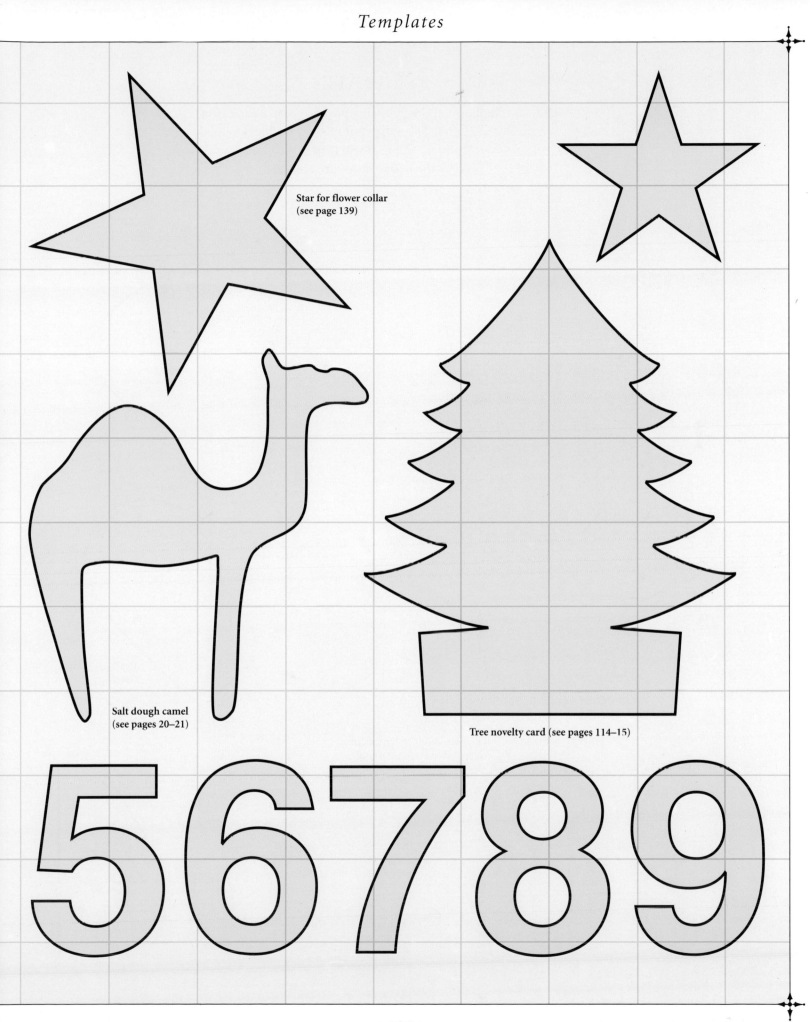

Star for flower collar
(see page 139)

Salt dough camel
(see pages 20–21)

Tree novelty card (see pages 114–15)

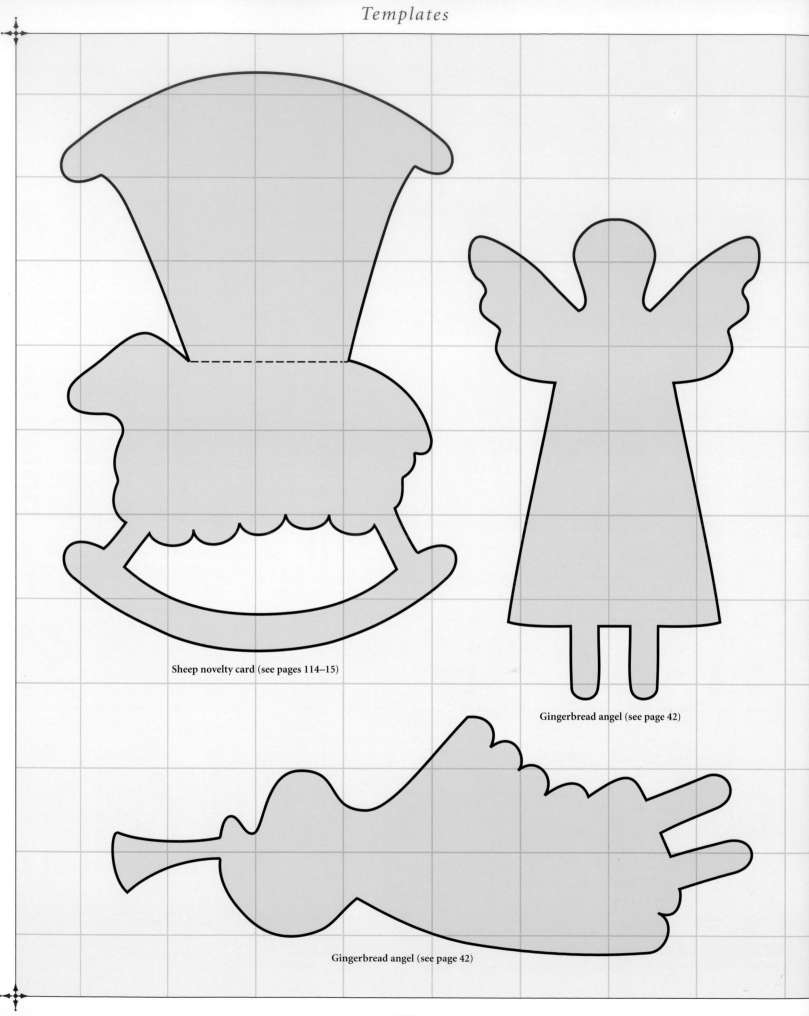

Sheep novelty card (see pages 114–15)

Gingerbread angel (see page 42)

Gingerbread angel (see page 42)

GINGERBREAD HOUSE (See page 181)

Assemble the house on a cake board, using royal icing to stick the pieces together. First form wall pieces B and C into a box shape. Pipe icing along the roof ridges of end pieces C and along the top of the roof pieces A, and press into position. Support roof overhang until dry, about 15 minutes.

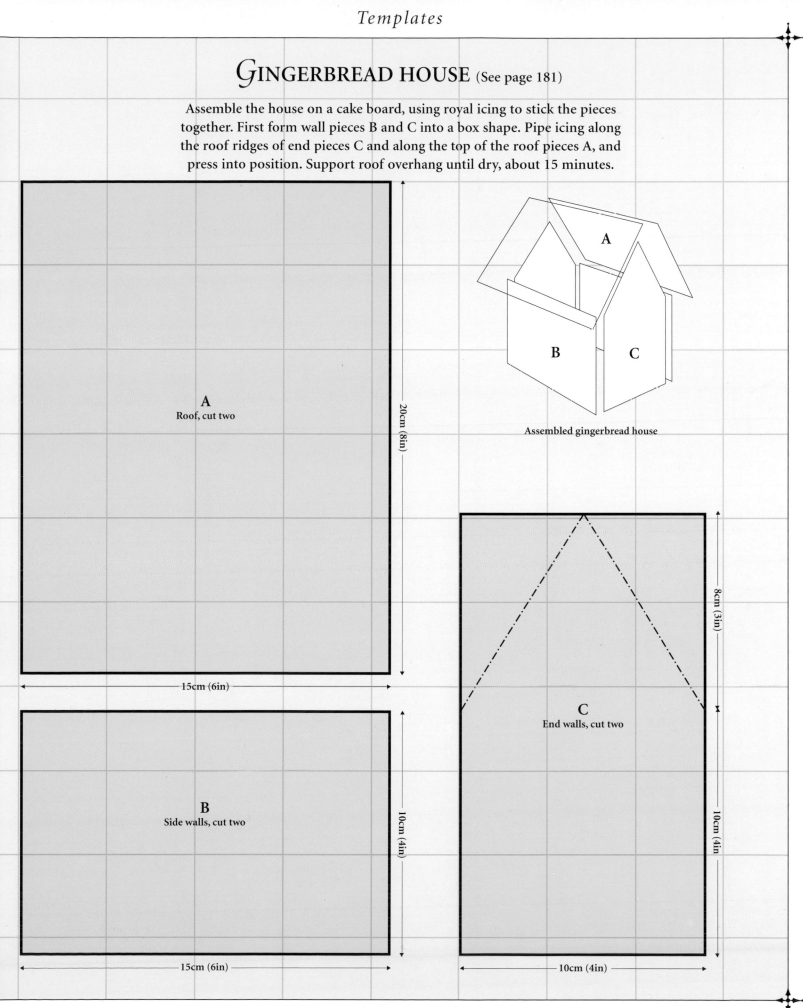

A
Roof, cut two

20cm (8in)

15cm (6in)

Assembled gingerbread house

B
Side walls, cut two

10cm (4in)

15cm (6in)

C
End walls, cut two

8cm (3in)

10cm (4in)

10cm (4in)

*I*NDEX